PREMONITIONS

and

PSYCHIC WARNINGS

Real Stories of Haunting Predictions

Edrick Thay

GHOST HOUSE

Ghost House Books

© 2005 by Ghost House Books
First printed in 2005 10 9 8 7 6 5 4 3 2 1
Printed in Canada

The Publisher: Ghost House Books
Distributed by Lone Pine Publishing
10145 – 81 Avenue
Edmonton, AB T6E 1W9
Canada

1808 – B Street NW, Suite 140
Auburn, WA 98001
USA

Website: http://www.ghostbooks.net

Library and Archives Canada Cataloguing in Publication

Thay, Edrick, 1977-
   Premonitions and psychic warnings / Edrick Thay.

ISBN 1-894877-58-6

   1. Parapsychology. 2. Ghosts. I. Title.
BF1031.T42 2005   130   C2005-902300-7

Editorial Director: Nancy Foulds
Project Editors: Carol Woo, Sandra Bit
Production Manager: Gene Longson
Book Design, Layout & Production: Trina Koscielnuk
Cover Design: Gerry Dotto

Photo Credits: Every effort has been made to accurately credit sources. Any errors or omissions should be directed to the publisher for changes in future editions. The images in this book are reproduced with the kind permission of the following sources: Istock (p. 12, 24: Diane Diederich; p. 47, 52: Piet Rijkhoff; p. 104: Bernd Klumpp; p. 130: Nicholas Belton; p. 164, 191: Mika Makkonen).

We acknowledge the financial support of the Government of Canada through the Book Publishing Industry Development Program (BPIDP) for our publishing activities.

PC: P5

To Barbara and Susie

Contents

Acknowledgments 6

Introduction 8

Chapter 1: Love and Death

Dial P for Psychic 13

Death Not For Him 17

I Dream of Father 22

From Beyond the Grave 26

Cloudy Skies 30

Asleep At The Table 37

Chronicle of An Accident Foretold 41

Chapter 2: Strangers Among Us

Mario's Arrival 48

The Touch 51

Cash to Go 55

Golf, Arizona and Sting 60

His Cheating Heart 65

Cabin Fever 69

Bringing Up Baby 75

Chapter 3: Help Is On The Way

Car Crash 81

9/11 85

Brotherly Love 90

Love Connection 96

Automatic Driving 102
How to Climb A Ladder 106
A Bright Light 116
Psychic Doodling 120

Chapter 4: Danger! Danger!

The Psychic Life 125
Party Premonition 134
Too Stubborn 136
Mother Knows Best 140
Father, Stay Home 143
Joyride 147
Baby Blues 150
A Skeptic No Longer 153
One Shirt, Two Shirt, Blue Shirt 158

Chapter 5: Farewell To Thee

A Mother's Farewell 165
A Death Foretold 169
A Grandfather Says Goodbye 172
Dance of the Fireflies 176
Mother, Mother 179
The Hitchhiker in the Road 183
Signs 188

Acknowledgments

There are countless individuals who deserve my eternal thanks and gratitude for this book. They shared openly, at great emotional cost, often on matters highly personal and grievous. Without their contributions, this book would be vastly thinner and considerably dull. Sadly, I cannot name many of them but take comfort in the fact that they know who they are and hope that they realize how deeply appreciative and grateful I truly am. I pray that I've done justice to your accounts.

I must also thank Michael J. Kouri for taking time away from his obviously busy schedule to speak with me. His interview proved fascinating and educational.

Thanks too go to my editor, Carol Woo, for her sure and judicious hand in reining in my tendency to ramble on at length. A nod goes to Nancy Foulds, whose writing advice proved invaluable and who put me in touch with Michael J. Kouri in the first place. I would also like to thank all at Ghost House Publishing. You've done, as ever, a wonderful job.

A special and huge thanks goes out to Barbara Garcia. I first met Barbara when writing *Haunted Cemeteries*, at which time she predicted that I would be writing a book on psychics within a year. I dismissed her prediction as there were other projects that needed my attention. She was, in the end, correct and I've learned over the months that she usually is. Barbara, your assistance was invaluable and, most of all, enlightening. Your generosity and integrity are second to none.

This book would simply not have been possible without you. You have my undying thanks.

Finally, I must, as always, thank those individuals who helped me smile when I felt overwhelmed and intimidated by this project. Gratitude goes to Carmen Rojas, Curt Pillipow, Bonnie Kar, Allan Mott (I promise to say hello to you the next time we're at The Savoy) and Dan Asfar. Thanks also to my family, especially my twin brother, Eldwin Thay, whose support over the last couple of months I could never fully repay.

Introduction

As a twin, one of the most common questions that I've been asked (after who's older, of course) is whether or not my twin and I have ever had a psychic experience. I assume it's a question borne out of the assumption that we're identical twins, split from one ovum and therefore blessed with a psychic connection. Alas, we're not. We're just two brothers who happened to share a womb and a dearth of psychic experiences. Of course, sharing the same zygotic ancestry is by no means necessary for individuals to experience premonitions and psychic warnings. All that is needed, it seems, is a shared connection with humanity, and an awareness of the life and energy that binds us and unites us in the struggle for existence. It requires faith and belief in a mystery that resists science and logic and that has fascinated people for millennia.

The ancient Greeks had their oracles, most memorably Clytemnestra, the princess doomed by Apollo to see the future but never to be believed. So too did the ancient Romans. In China, fortune-tellers have been divining the future for centuries, reading facial features, palms and in what may be the oldest known method of fortune-telling in the world, using Kau Chime, a set of 78 numbered bamboo sticks held in a bamboo case, to offer a glimpse of the future and its myriad of possibilities. In this way, modern societies are little different from their forebears. We still look for omens and signs; we still cling to traditions and rituals believed to possess the influence to affect the future. Why do we read horoscopes? Why do we not walk under a ladder? Why do we have lucky charms? Like our ancestral forebears, we shy away from uncertainty and gravitate towards control. Knowing the future gives us agency and control of our destinies. Foreknowledge is seductive, tempting and alluring. Ironically enough, psychics, such as Barbara Garcia and Michael J. Kouri, recoil from the notion that all a psychic does is predict the future.

True psychics do not deal strictly with divination. Certainly, they do offer visions of the future, but by no means is that future set. Rather, psychics see themselves as guides, offering direction and advice on how best both to actualize an individual's potential and to interpret the signposts along the avenue of life. It's a subtle difference, but a difference nonetheless, and one with great consequences. Take the stories of Ariana and Charlotte, women from vastly different walks of life who both sought out Barbara Garcia for answers about their love lives, their careers and their families. Answers they received and so much more. Their consciousnesses were altered, and their lives irrevocably changed for the better. They'd all been to psychics before but had never experienced anything so visceral, enlightening and real.

Reality. When I began researching this book, I was expecting to write grand and operatic stories about averted tragedies, disasters and crimes. The reality of it all was that these accounts are rare. The sort of grand, soaring and mysterious predictions of soothsayers like Nostradamus and Edgar Cayce are, of course, fascinating and thrilling, and it's clear why both individuals have become figures shrouded in legend and myth. But, for the most part, the accounts I uncovered through dozens of interviews are small and highly personal. It's in their specificity that their universal appeal lies. Who, after all, has not known a loss, like Sunny's in *A Mother's Farewell*? Who has not known the heartbreak of a lost love like Chloe's in *Dial P for Psychic*? I've chosen to focus on accounts such as these because they are about individuals who, like everyone else, are seeking a means to manage their sometimes unruly lives.

Of course, there are stories here too where a premonition has given an individual the ability to alter a possibly disastrous future as in *Automatic Driving* and *Joyride*. Others may be impossibly grim, where individuals have been given a vision of an immutable future. Try as they might, they're unable to change the future for the better at all. It happened to Teddy in *Father, Stay Home* and to a devastated family in *Signs*. Omens, signs and premonitions abound in these accounts.

All of the following stories are true, in so far as they are based on interviews with individuals who, to the best of their knowledge and mine, claimed that these events actually happened. Most of the people I interviewed requested anonymity, a trend that speaks loudly to the stigma that psychics and the world of psychic phenomena often unfairly bear, and in those cases, their names have been changed. In some accounts, not only have names been changed, but also dates and places that may have rendered transparent the cloak of anonymity. As such, I do not present these stories as irrefutable and empirical evidence of the psychic world. In the end, these are just stories, which will prove, I hope, entertaining at the very least, and enlightening at the very best. Take them, if you prefer, as snapshots and portraits of the wonders and mysteries of human existence.

Psychics speak often of trying to bring light into a world that is increasingly dark, hateful and uncertain. I am not so bold as to claim that I have done or even attempted the same. Rather, I hope to have shed light on a subject that is all too often sceptically and callously dismissed and derided.

1
Love and Death

Dial P for Psychic

Love and career. These are the things people care about. These are the things people want to know about. How many times have you been asked, "Are you seeing anyone?" or "How're things going with [insert name here]?" Probably about as many times as you've inquired, "How's work going?" and wondered of a new acquaintance, "What do you do?" You would, of course, then know the anxiety these questions can sometimes provoke. What if you're confused about your career? Or your relationship? For Chloe, these sort of questions brought forth the concerns and misgivings she had about both her love life and career. She really didn't know what to do with either of them and decided that she was going to need some help of a psychic nature.

Chloe had consulted many psychics before. But each time, she had grown wary and suspicious of their alleged abilities. In the end, they always asked more questions than they answered, a fact that struck a discordant note with Chloe. "You're the psychic," she would say irritably, "why don't you tell me?" It was a simple question, but her psychics must have assumed it was rhetorical and left it unanswered. So it was with Chloe in the fall of 2003: without a psychic and desperately in need of guidance and assurance. On the recommendation of a friend, she turned to Barbara Garcia.

Chloe had just ended her relationship with her boyfriend, but was left, in the aftermath, wondering if she had done the right thing. After all, she was, by her own admission, still very much in love with him and had only ended the relationship because she was tired of being pushed away and felt he needed time alone and space to deal with the family tragedies that had led to his withdrawal. She was in turmoil. It all dovetailed nicely with the questions she had concerning her career.

After two and a half years at a film production company, Chloe had yet to be promoted and she didn't know why. She had worked hard, much harder than the pretty girls who had come in flashing their brilliantly white smiles and who left when the stresses of the job required more than they could handle. Her disillusionment had her questioning her loyalty to the company, and she wondered if it wasn't time for her to leave and do something else. She had had other lucrative job offers, but unfortunately, they hadn't meshed with her career ambitions. She wanted to work in film, not television. It was a stressful time, to say the least.

Chloe went to her first reading with Barbara with trepidation. But after the reading, Chloe was no longer dubious. "What was impressive," Chloe says, "was that she dealt with facts." No sooner had Chloe sat down than Barbara looked at her and said, "You let someone go within the last few days." Barbara went on to describe, in intimate details, the particulars of the relationship that she couldn't possibly have known: the death of the boyfriend's grandparents and his aunt's recent diagnosis of terminal lung cancer. "I hadn't told her a thing at that point," Chloe says, amazed. "She nailed every single detail." Most importantly, the reading gave Chloe the confidence to accept her decision to break up with her boyfriend and allowed her to remain optimistic for the future. While he wouldn't be in her life in the near future, Barbara saw the possibility of reconciliation. Chloe still felt as if she had abandoned him, but Barbara assured her that she had done the right thing.

As far as her career, Barbara had more good news. She advised patience. "They're grooming you," she said, "and in four weeks, you're going to be approached about something involving the co-owner." Still, Chloe maintained her caution. The claims seemed preposterous and Chloe was sure that Barbara was more than a little off. Four weeks later, Chloe's doubts proved to be wrong.

A manager at the company told her that she was indeed in line for a promotion, one that would involve working closely with, surprise, surprise, the co-owner of the company. "It freaked me out," Chloe recalls. "It really did. It hit me and I was like, 'Oh my God. *This* is what she's talking about.'" The next day, Chloe met with the director. He asked, plainly, "You want to come work with me?" Chloe was ecstatic and answered in the overwhelmingly positive. She often thought of what might have happened if she hadn't stayed patient, as Barbara had advised. She may very well have taken one of the jobs that had been offered to her—which, in Chloe's words, "would have been a tragedy." Professionally, Chloe has never been more content. Her love life, on the other hand, was another matter entirely.

At the first reading, Barbara had told Chloe that "a big move was going to affect her life in three months." Of everything that Barbara had said, Chloe had found this cryptic prediction the most implausible. She had no plans to move, loved Los Angeles and now, months later, with her promotion, the idea of a move seemed absolutely ridiculous.

But, at the end of February 2004, with matters between them still unresolved, Chloe's ex-boyfriend called her. He had devastating news. Because of a new job, he would be moving away from Los Angeles; Barbara's prediction had come true. In trying to decipher the meaning of Barbara's words, Chloe had never considered the possibility that the big move might apply to someone else in her life. For weeks, Chloe was depressed and she wondered just how seriously this move would affect her life. Barbara did her best to ease Chloe's anxiety, calmly predicting that reconciliation and perhaps even marriage awaited. The news was like a salve and so, too, was the move. It affected Chloe's life for the positive.

The distance allowed Chloe's heart to heal. "Out of sight, out of mind," Chloe says. Although the old adage may seem pithy and cruel, Chloe states it without any malice. She realized that the move allowed her to focus on the parts of her life she was able to control. "I was scared to let him go," she says, "but the move helped. It healed me and made me stronger. I've more serenity in my life now." She credits Barbara for all of that and more. "My life has been more peaceful since I met her," says Chloe. "A lot of things are clearer to me because of her."

Death Not For Him

Jacob had always had a fascination with the psychic world. He read often about famous psychics like Edgar Cayce, Jeanne Dixon and the icon of them all, Nostradamus. When he was old enough, he began taking the bus and the train from his parents' house in Cicero to downtown Chicago where he would visit any and all the psychics he could find. Over time, he grew somewhat disillusioned as he realized that most of the psychics he found were inefficient, vague and worst of all, woefully inaccurate. But it all changed one day last year when Jacob came across a musty little shop in Chinatown. Its flickering neon sign beckoned him to enter.

Inside, he encountered a handsome older woman, whose practice seemed much less complicated and showy than the ones he'd seen previously. Absent were the crystal balls, tarot cards and Ouija boards that had been staples of every other psychic he had seen. Instead, the woman just sat at a small table, staring beatifically at whoever happened to drop by. Jacob knew that he'd found a true psychic. He couldn't explain it, but he just felt something that stirred his soul.

After a 15-minute session, Jacob was grateful, at long last, that his instincts had led him here. The psychic spent most of the session not predicting the future but telling Jacob about himself and his family. She knew immediately about his fractured relationship with both his mother and father. She knew that his grandmother constantly hounded him to find a better job and to make more money and that his mother and father were pressing him to drop his music program to take up law or medicine. She divined how guilty he felt about his decisions, how small he became whenever his successful, older sister with the six-figure salary in New York City came to visit. Jacob was astonished by her accuracy. At the end, the psychic predicted that someone in his family was going to die and very soon.

The news wasn't exactly a surprise. Jacob's maternal grandfather was very ill and had been for a long time. In fact, just the week before, he had been coughing up blood. When his grandmother found him sprawled out on the bathroom floor, he was immediately rushed to the hospital. Doctors had found a rupture in his lung and were trying to understand why it had happened.

His grandfather was still in the hospital, his body growing increasingly frail. He slept in fits and starts, and in just a few days, was simply miserable. He cursed at the nurses, and the only time he became less agitated was when family came to visit. All he wanted to do was to go home, but Jacob wasn't even sure that would ever happen. No one was, actually.

Still, as ready as Jacob was to bid farewell to his grandfather, the psychic's prediction somehow made the whole thing easier to bear. Jacob began to spend more time with his grandfather, even though it was hard to see how frail the older man had become. He snuck in his grandfather's favorite snacks, crackers and French fries, and fed him surreptitiously, always with an eye out for any disapproving nurses.

He sat there, maintaining his vigil, as friends and relatives arrived in greater numbers every day. Jacob marveled at his grandfather's memory—the faces he recognized and

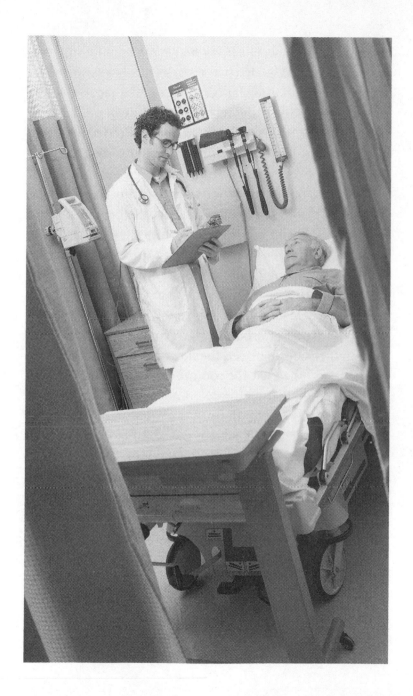

the names he knew. His body may have been failing him, but his mind was as sharp as ever, so Jacob was surprised when his grandfather failed to recognize Jacob's young cousin, Jessica. She had long been a favorite of both grandparents, so the family nicknamed her #1. Pretty, intelligent and funny, she had won their hearts and was still the recipient of their extravagant Christmas and birthday presents.

His grandfather grew increasingly confused, as though he couldn't even see Jessica standing before him. Jacob prodded his grandfather and told him that #1 was there, but his grandfather just moaned and groaned and tossed on the bed in an agitated fit. His grandfather spoke cryptically in his broken English, and Jacob could only discern the words, "Death is coming." Jessica stood there awkwardly, unsure of what to do. Finally, she kissed her grandfather's head, placed the flowers she had brought on the table and then left the room.

The grandfather continued mumbling, "Death is coming," over and over again until the nurses finally sedated him. Jacob was frightened. His grandfather knew his own death was on its way. Or so Jacob thought.

A couple of days later, the family received the news. The grandfather would be all right. Well, sort of. He had chronic pneumonia and would need to take medication, but he would be all right. Jacob was relieved, but somewhat puzzled by his psychic's prediction. Could his psychic have been wrong?

When Jacob visited his grandfather at his home, the grandfather repeatedly asked about Jessica. Jacob reassured him each time that she was fine. "Something terrible is going to happen," the grandfather said ominously.

The psychic and Jacob's grandfather were both correct. There was indeed a death in Jacob's family, but not who Jacob had expected at all. He learned that Jessica had been killed in a car accident on her way to visit some friends in Indiana. Death had come for his sweet cousin, not his grandfather. It was her death that the grandfather and the psychic had foreseen. In his delirium, Jacob's grandfather was unable to recognize or see Jessica at the hospital because she had been draped in the shroud of death, not long for the earth. When his grandfather heard the news, he just nodded, sat down wearily and closed his eyes. He had seen enough.

I Dream of Father

When Elly was just a young girl in the early 1960s, her world was idyllic. She spent nights curled up in her father's lap, and she would hold his hand, marveling at how small hers seemed when wrapped in his long, slender fingers.

When he kissed her goodnight, his stubble was coarse and rough, but she came to love and savor its grittiness, just as he loved the smooth and supple touch of her rosy cheeks. The sensations were electric, pulsing with compassion and tenderness. It was what she missed most when her father fell ill, crippled with a bad heart that just didn't care how much love it was capable of possessing. His condition was so terrible that he had to be hospitalized. Nights were empty now. Her father's spot on the couch remained unoccupied. She went to bed, scared and confused, without his calming and reassuring touch.

When she saw her father, it was devastating. He was in a place that smelled nothing like him, his scent obliterated by the caustic and stinging aroma of bleach. The green walls and linoleum floors were cold and sterile, hardly the place for her father, who now looked like something out of a science-fiction novel, with tubes and machines connected to his body. After that first visit, she was so upset that her mother decided it best not to visit him in the room. Instead, they spent their daily evening visits in the visiting room, anxiously waiting for a nurse to wheel Elly's father out in a wheelchair. The visit was too brief for her. Every night, when vistors' hours were over, she pleaded with her mother for more time, for just one more minute.

Elly didn't care about the rules and regulations. She just wanted to stay with her father.

After three months, Elly began to despair. There was a marked change in her mood and her mother gently pressed her to tell her why. "Daddy is going to die," she said. Her mother, who was struggling with her own fears about losing her husband, told Elly that her father was strong and with the best doctors, he would continue to fight. She didn't tell Elly that her husband had pulled her aside one night and whispered into her ear, "Take good care of Elly. Take care of our little girl and our baby."

But Elly couldn't be persuaded. She cried until early in the morning, only resting when the exhaustion of her constant grief became too much to bear. Her mother continued to reassure her, but Elly remained adamant. "Daddy is going to die," she insisted. "Why do you say that?" her mother asked. "How do you know?" Elly looked her mother in the eye and whispered, "Because I saw him. I saw Daddy's funeral." The vision had come to her in a dream one September morning so vivid and real that she had woken up with tears in her eyes.

In the dream, she remembered a preacher uttering a final prayer. There were flowers all around the grave—lilies, irises, roses. Their sweet scents mingled with the crisp fall air. Her mother's hand rested on her shoulder while she watched the earth swallow her father's casket, and then her mother turned her around and led her away. In the mirror-like surface of their black car, she saw her brother and her navy blue dress, with its white and blue stripes. Her small feet were tucked into their white socks and navy shoes. All around her, as far as her eyes could

The flowers around the grave looked all too familiar to Elly.

see, were grey and black tombstones. "Time to go home, honey," her mother said, offering Elly her hand. They began walking slowly towards the cemetery gates. Elly felt as though everyone was staring at her, watching and waiting to help in case she faltered. As they passed through the wrought-iron cemetery gates, Elly woke.

Not a day went by that Elly didn't think about the dream. It stalked her every step, lurked in her imagination and prowled her sleep. She knew her father was going to die. She just knew it. But she had no idea when he was going to leave her. Every morning she woke up hoping and praying that this day, at least, wouldn't be the day and that she would get to see him, just one last time, in the evening.

Three weeks after the day she had her dream, Elly woke up. It was a bright, shiny Tuesday. Her room was awash with sunlight, but basked as she was in the sun's warm yellow glow, something didn't feel right. The light in the room was almost too harsh, as if everything had been drained a little of its color and brilliance. It was already 8:30 AM, so Elly was late for school. Her mother usually woke her up so she would have time for breakfast, but today, everything was quiet.

Elly padded out of her room into a darkened hallway. She walked towards the kitchen door, aware now that something was very wrong. Behind it, she could hear voices. A lot of voices. Her aunt and her mother were sniffling and crying. With a quivering hand, she pushed the door open. Her aunt just looked at her and said, "Come to me, Elly. Your daddy's gone home with Jesus." Elly ran into her outstretched arms and wept.

The next few days passed by in a great haze. Elly can remember her mother picking out a casket and her cousin dragging her into the funeral home to look at her father lying so peacefully in his casket and running screaming from the building. And she remembers the funeral was exactly as she had seen in her dream three weeks before. Elly and her mother walked through the same cemetery gates, only this time, it wasn't a dream.

Elly still loves and misses her father deeply and though her memories of him are few, they are precious. She can still recall the feel of his stubble against her cheek, the smooth touch of his long, slender fingers. At night, when she sleeps, she is with him again. He comes to her, in her dreams.

From Beyond The Grave

Julia was positive that she had found the love of her life. They had met during their first week at college, during a dormitory orientation in a small, cramped common room on her floor. He had been sitting next to her and had introduced himself. It wasn't long before she learned that he hailed from her hometown of Atlanta. She hadn't expected to meet anyone all the way from Georgia in Colorado, but her connection with Russell was immediate. It wasn't long before they became more than just friends.

They dated steadily throughout the year, and though they spent the summer apart working in separate cities, their love continued to bloom. They exchanged countless letters, sent novels back and forth. As the summer ended, Julia was thrilled at the idea of returning to Colorado. She and Russell moved out of their dorms and found off-campus homes with their friends. The year seemed full of endless possibilities. It wasn't to be, however.

Shortly before classes were scheduled to start, Julia knew that something was wrong when she and Russell hadn't spoken for days. It was unusual. Not a night had gone by where they hadn't said goodnight to each other until now. She e-mailed him and called him, but couldn't leave a message because his answering machine was full. Concerned, Julia called his parents in Atlanta. The heaviness in his mother's usually buoyant voice was obvious, and Julia sensed that something dreadful had happened.

Through a voice choked with sobs, Russell's mother told Julia the devastating news. "I felt as if I had been shot," Julia recalls. Russell was dead. He had been driving home one evening, passing through an intersection. Russell had the green light, but a drunk driver ran the red light and crashed into him. Russell's car was almost cut in half. He died en route to the hospital. Julia was numb. She remembers nothing else after that moment.

Though she was due back at Colorado in just a couple of weeks, Julia chose to return instead to Atlanta. She couldn't bear the idea of being back in a place where everything she saw—every building, every street, every person—would remind her of Russell. "I was hopelessly in love with him," Julia says. "I couldn't return. It would have been too hard." Instead, she returned to her parents' house and spent weeks grieving in her bedroom. Though her parents urged her to attend both Russell's funeral and his wake, Julia refused. She wasn't ready to say good-bye. The next few months passed by at a glacial pace. For Julia, everything seemed to have been drained of any real significance.

Most days, she found it an effort just to get out of bed. She would often snap at her mother and father whenever they came to check up on her. She ate little, and she became increasingly withdrawn. Nights were her refuge, and she considered herself lucky if she happened to dream of Russell. For months, Julia sunk ever deeper into her depression. Her parents wanted her to see a therapist and maybe think about returning to college, but Julia resisted.

Julia had dreamt of Russell often and prayed every night that she would see him. One evening, Russell did one better. He actually appeared before her. Julia was sleeping when a bright light roused her from her slumber. Her entire room was bathed in a soft white glow. The light didn't sting Julia's eyes. Instead, it enveloped her, and she remembers feeling an extraordinary sense of calm and peace. From deep within the bank of light, she saw a figure emerge. It was Russell and he looked exactly as she remembered, handsome in an unconventional way. He wore the same dark suit that he had worn for one of their campus formals. She had always loved the way he looked in it.

He sat on her bed and Julia was amazed that she could feel the mattress sag beneath him. His spirit was in her room. He smiled and told Julia that he had come to help. "You need to stop feeling so bad," he said. It broke her heart to hear his voice once again. "I've been watching you, Julia. You can't keep beating yourself up," he continued. "It kills me to see you like this. You have to move on because life has so much in store for you," he pleaded. "I have to go now, but you will feel better in the morning. You will move on." With those words, Julia's boyfriend vanished from her room. For a moment, she sat in her bed, wondering if she had really seen him or if she had just imagined it all.

When she woke in the morning, it was as if a veil had been brushed away from her face. She didn't feel happy exactly, but she certainly felt much better than she had in months. It was as if she could finally breathe again. She wondered if it really had been Russell who had visited her the night before.

When she told her parents about his visit, they were far from surprised. She learned that Russell had appeared to them as well, offering dire warnings. He had told them that she had planned on killing herself with pills and that if he couldn't save her, they would have to intervene. Julia realized that their love had survived even death and with that reassurance in mind, she resolved to conquer her depression.

Julia waited out the end of the winter semester, and then spent her summer working and traveling. The entire time she felt Russell with her and took solace in her belief that he was all right, wherever he was, and that in time, they would meet again. She knows how crazy it all sounds, but she truly believes that Russell saved her life. "I don't know where I was headed," she says, "but another couple of months and I don't think I could have taken much more of the depression. He felt my pain and he came to me. He saved me." Julia returned to school and though it was difficult, she managed to complete her degree. She has her life back, and still occasionally, she thinks of Russell.

Cloudy Skies

Mo Hainer was always surrounded by psychics. When she was a young child, she realized that the gift of foresight was particularly strong in her mother. As she grew older, she learned that it wasn't just her mother's skill. Her sister, Ruth Ann, was blessed with psychic abilities of her own. Mo was too. But as extraordinarily gifted as each of these women were, it seemed that they were clueless when it came to divining answers about their own futures. Interestingly enough, psychics seem be able to predict the triumphs and tragedies of the people who consult them, but their own lives remain inscrutable. Mo had spent many years of her youth and adulthood tuned into the lives of those around her, but she knew "how hard it was to be intuitive about your own family."

Mo first heard about Barbara Garcia in the late 1970s when she was attending a lecture about automatic writing, for which Barbara was already renowned. Automatic writing is a process in which a psychic enters a state of altered consciousness and begins to write, or in some cases, to draw visions of the future. Barbara's automatic drawing played a part in bringing the Hillside Strangler of Los Angeles to justice, and she was now involved in providing comfort to members of the organization, Parents of Murdered Children. Mo turned to Barbara's automatic drawing when she decided that she needed the guidance of a psychic who wasn't related to her.

At their first reading together, Barbara simply concentrated on Mo's name, focusing on her energy and soul.

With a pencil in hand, she moved over a large sheet of paper laid out in front of her. At first, all Mo could see were just a few lines, here and there, looking like nothing but random scribbles. But as the lines merged together, they began forming two recognizable shapes, like ships emerging from a bank of fog. When Barbara finished, Mo took a closer look at what had emerged. Mo found herself looking at "two dark clouds, with one bigger than the other." *What could it all mean,* Mo wondered. The clouds certainly looked ominous. They reminded her of the black, rolling clouds that swept across the Minnesota sky of her childhood, unleashing their fury in thunderstorms. The very look of them chilled her heart.

Barbara's face was inscrutable during the reading, but when she spoke, it was with much gravity tempered with optimism and warmth. "I liked the way she read," Mo says. "She's caring and compassionate and encouraging." Barbara explained how the dark clouds represented two crises that would engulf Mo's life very soon—but also that there was no need to worry. The clouds did have a silver lining, after all, and Mo would find her way out of the darkness. Mo had very few specifics to go on, but when her life began to spiral, she had an epiphany—these were the clouds that Barbara had seen. One cloud symbolized a rift with her family; the larger, darker one symbolized something far more ominous concerning her daughter.

At 56, Mo had decided to go back to school to obtain a master's degree. As she learned more about herself and developed more confidence in who and what she was, she found that she related less and less with her circle of friends. "I changed," she says. "Life is all about changing.

I began seeking people out who were more like-minded." It was a change that her family found, at first, jarring and difficult to accommodate. She was moving and growing away from them, and it was an awkward transition. When asked to describe what happened in detail, Mo, normally open and talkative, becomes hesitant, as if the memories are too difficult to relive. She explains her reluctance, saying that the particulars "are just too big a hassle to get through." Instead, she happily points to the conclusion that Barbara had predicted all along. As the years passed, Mo and her family slowly but surely bridged the gap that once separated them. Mo is now 74 and she is once again close to her sister, Ruth Ann. When they speak together, it's with an ease and intuition borne from not just their shared psychic abilities, but also from two people who are only too well aware of how close they came to losing their loved ones.

While her estrangement from her family was distressing, the tragedy of her daughter, the other bigger black cloud, was devastating. Mo can recall the events that took place over 20 years ago as though they had just happened. The memories are always there. In 1982, Mo's daughter became ill. Mo suspected something was wrong, but couldn't have known exactly how wrong everything was. She could see that her daughter was out of sorts, unable to focus or concentrate on any task for very long. Her daughter had no appetite for food. She pecked at her plate as if she were a bird, eating little, as if the food was repulsive. Mo was shaken by her daughter's nausea and vomiting, but she hoped that the illness would run its course in due time. It didn't. With an alarming and terrifying swiftness, her condition worsened. Her daughter seemed confused and lost and complained often of exhaustion and feeling chilled even on the hottest and muggiest of days. Her hands and legs swelled and began resembling fleshy balloons. Concerned, Mo insisted that her daughter see a doctor. The diagnosis was not good. Her daughter wasn't just sick; she was dying. She was only 26.

Both her kidneys, for whatever reason, were failing and poisoning her body. Doctors immediately placed her under their care, hooking her up to dialysis machines and all sorts of other equipment that could not replicate what it had taken nature eons to perfect. Doctors told Mo that they "didn't know if her kidneys would ever function on their own again." Mo tried hard to bolster herself with Barbara's optimism, but seeing her daughter tethered to all those machines, she wondered if her daughter would ever live to see her 27th birthday. The doctors did everything they could, including preparing Mo for the real possibility that her daughter was going to die. Barbara remained staunch in her belief that Mo's daughter would recover.

Mo visited her daughter often, and it was as if death had already taken parts of her away. "She was pretty incoherent," Mo recalls. There were lucid moments, of course. One evening, as Mo watched her daughter lying helplessly on her hospital bed, she asked her daughter, "Do you remember how you always said that you were going to die young?" With tears in her eyes, the daughter nodded. Mo continued and it surely must have broken her heart to do so. She choked out the words, "I think you're going to die young." "But I don't want to die," her daughter wailed.

The tears cascaded down her cheeks. "I want to live until I'm in my 80s."

It was a sublime moment, the moment when Mo's daughter "became awake. She was choosing to stay." Mo could feel renewed strength and vigor coursing through her daughter's body, almost as if it had become an entity all its own, filling the hospital room with its energy and power. Her daughter claimed that she could feel a spirit in the room. But for the next two weeks, her daughter's kidneys continued to lie dormant, and doctors told Mo that nothing else could be done, that she was beyond their help. Despite this, Mo believed in what Barbara told her and the impossible happened. In Mo's words, "it was a miracle." Her daughter's kidneys began to function again.

For a month, her daughter's life had hovered precariously between life and death, edging ever closer to oblivion. Every medical official who had seen her had predicted death. Only Barbara had predicted life. "Barbara was right," Mo says. "She saw the big, black cloud but knew that a miracle would happen." Twenty-two years later, Mo's daughter's kidneys function at almost 100 percent efficiency. It would not be the last time that Barbara would defy medical opinion and be proven correct.

When Mo's daughter wanted to have a child, doctors warned against it. Pregnancy could adversely affect her already weakened kidneys and could cost her life. It just was a risk her doctors were not willing to allow her to take. Barbara allowed that there might be medical risks, but told Mo that if her daughter became pregnant, she foresaw no complications at all. Both mother and child would be fine. Mo's daughter, wanting nothing more than to be a mother, chose to have a child despite the dire warnings. Mo became a grandmother to a healthy baby girl.

"Barbara has been such a blessing," Mo says. "She really helped me a lot with my daughters." And not just in health matters. At one reading, Mo asked Barbara a question that had been plaguing her for a while. Her instincts were telling her that one of her daughters would become a widow. She didn't really want to know whether her instincts were correct, but if she was, she wanted her daughter to be prepared. The daughter didn't have much money, relying largely upon her husband's income.

Mo's intuition was correct. Barbara saw one of her daughters wearing a veil, but Barbara was unable to pinpoint exactly when Mo's son-in-law would die. She only predicted that he would be young. And though Barbara couldn't tell Mo with any certainty which daughter it would be, she had her suspicions and they meshed perfectly with Mo's. One of her daughters had married a man with deeply rooted problems that surfaced only after they had wed. The husband was an alcoholic and "it caused all sorts of problems," not the least of which was its adverse effect upon his liver. Diseased and bloated, his liver was beginning to fail. After hearing Barbara's prediction, Mo pressed her daughter to buy life insurance. A short while later, her husband succumbed to liver disease. He was in his early 40s.

Barbara saw divorce for another of Mo's daughters. For Mo, the premonition was probably treated as good news. "She had a very bad relationship with him," Mo says. "He was abusive. I'm not sure that it was physical, but it was definitely emotional and mental." Mo felt powerless to help. Her daughter was with this man for over a decade and no end seemed to be in sight. But Barbara saw things differently. She saw Mo's daughter married to another man, someone who "would be tanned, short and quiet and the exact opposite of her current husband."

Amazingly, a year later, Mo's daughter divorced her husband. A short time later, she met a man who was tanned, short and quiet. Initially, her daughter didn't care for the man romantically, but he had taken a liking to her and persisted. As time went on, Mo's daughter found herself growing attached. He was good to her, contributing positively to her life. They married, and in Mo's words, "He's been good for her. They're extremely compatible and they're very much still in love."

Mo credits Barbara for her good fortune, saying that "the psychic has been an absolute treasure. She gives you hope." Even after 30 years of friendship, Mo says that Barbara continues to surprise her. Recently, Barbara told Mo that she saw her traveling to China to speak before a large group. "I couldn't believe it when she told me," Mo says excitedly. "But guess what? Ten months later, I got a letter from a counseling company I work with, and they asked me to go to China to speak." She's going to make the trip next fall. "I've done well," Mo says. When she says it, she's thinking of all that Barbara has done, not just for her, but for her family as well.

Asleep At The Table

Though Charlotte is now 30, happily married with two sons, she still often thinks of her grandfather and the peculiar circumstances surrounding his death. Although her grandfather died over two decades ago, to Charlotte, it's as if no time has passed at all. It's not often, after all, that you see your grandfather's death before it actually happens.

Charlotte had always been close to her grandfather. Her grandmother had passed away long before she was born, so her mother and father took care of her grandfather. They even moved to a new house just so that he could have a bedroom on the main floor because his weak knees made it difficult to handle the stairs. The baby Charlotte took a quick liking to her grandfather, who amused her endlessly with a mix of funny faces, games of peek-a-boo and stories. He brought her candy from his daily walks to the corner store, sneaking it to her when her parents weren't watching. But then one day, it all ended. Charlotte was nine and, suddenly, her grandfather just wasn't around anymore.

When she asked her mother and father to tell her what had happened to him, they did their best to explain it to her, but it was beyond her understanding. They talked about something called a stroke and how he would be home soon, but that he would be a little different. She smiled happily, hearing only how he would be home soon. He couldn't be that different, could he?

Her grandfather returned to the house weeks later, and to her dismay, Charlotte remembers that she recoiled a little when she first heard him speak. She couldn't understand a word he was saying; it was as if his mouth were full of marbles. He no longer went on his walks to the corner store, choosing instead to pass his days on the porch swing, staring out at the distant scenery behind their home. Charlotte withdrew too. He was different. Very different.

But then, her grandfather started disappearing for hours at a time during the day. And she noticed that her mother was around the house a lot more, cajoling and prodding her reluctant grandfather to go to something called rehab. Charlotte didn't know what the word meant, but little by little, rehab, and whatever it entailed, seemed to make her grandfather better. He no longer spoke as if his tongue had turned to mush, and with the aid of a cane, he was able, once again, to walk to the corner store and bring back the sugary sweets that Charlotte loved so much.

The house seemed to breathe a sigh of relief. The fog that had settled over everyone had lifted and her mother and father began laughing again. "He's going to be all right," her mother whispered to Charlotte one evening before tucking her into bed. "Everything's going to be fine." Charlotte had never even considered that it wouldn't be. A year came and went, and her grandfather's stroke became a distant memory. He sat beside her, as he always had, on her birthday and helped her blow out the 10 candles on her cake. Ten candles... her grandfather told her that she would soon be a young lady with too little time for an old relative like him. She told him that he was just being a big silly. Looking back, Charlotte feels that her grandfather knew that his time was near and was, in his own way, saying goodbye.

It was about a month after her 10th birthday. Charlotte's grandfather read to her from *Charlotte's Web*. Her mother tucked her in. Her father kissed her good-night. And then she slept. And as she slept, she dreamt. In her dream, she saw her grandfather asleep at the dinner table. She remembers poking him, trying to wake him up, but, like Rip van Winkle, he couldn't be stirred. When she woke, she just lay there in her bed, marveling at how real the dream had felt.

Charlotte had had vivid dreams before. But there was something about this one that refused to let her go. Something about it disturbed her, but she just didn't know what. All day long at school, the dream played like an endless loop in her head—through math, through English, through social studies. It bothered her so much that she even told her best friend.

That night, before going to sleep, Charlotte told her parents about the dream. Her mother was happy that she had told them about it. "Talking about a bad dream," she had said, "is the only way to make sure that it doesn't come back." It was good advice for Charlotte. She slept peacefully through the night and quickly forgot about the dream. If only her mother had something to prevent bad dreams from coming true.

Two nights later, Charlotte's family was gathered around the dinner table. It was a simple dinner of meat-loaf, green beans and mashed potatoes. Something about it all seemed eerily familiar to Charlotte. Hadn't she been eating meatloaf and mashed potatoes in her dream? Hadn't her grandfather been wearing the same green sweater? Hadn't Daisy, the family dog, been barking outside? Charlotte dismissed it all with a shake of her head and continued to eat. But then, she noticed that her grandfather wasn't eating, and his fork clattered to the ground. She prodded him, but he wouldn't stir. It was as if he had fallen asleep. It was just like her dream, save for one difference. There was sense of dread that she saw mirrored in the eyes of her parents. Her mother and father exchanged quick glances and before she knew what was happening, her father had swept her from the room. Her grandfather was dead.

Twenty years later, Charlotte still thinks about that dream. She sometimes wonders whether it was all just a cosmic coincidence and yes, there are days when she questions if she could have done something to avert his death. The guilt is omnipresent, but when it becomes too much to bear, she tells herself that she was only a little girl, just a child. She looks into her children's faces and knows that her grandfather lives on in them.

Chronicle of An Accident Foretold

Though it has been many years since the event, George can still recall it with great clarity. He speaks with a voice laden with regret and dread. Sometimes he wonders if he could have done anything. It's at times like these that he retreats from the world, accompanied only by guilt over his inaction and by a host of questions beginning with "what if." He tells himself that he was only a small child, too young to have understood what he saw in his dreams. It's a small comfort.

When George was a child, he spent many summer afternoons at his aunt's house. His mother and father worked often and since his aunt, a stay-at-home mother, had a son about George's age, it just made sense for him to be in his aunt's care. They all lived in the same neighborhood too, and the two children had been close from the time that they had been babies. Often, it became more than a chore just to get George to come home. He'd often beg to sleep over and if he couldn't stay, then he'd ask if his cousin Chris could stay over instead. They spent long nights together, staying up until the early hours of the morning, crawling in and around forts they'd construct out of their pillows, blankets and desk chairs. Sometimes, they'd sneak out into the night and explore the neighborhood that was familiar by day but became mysterious and unknown by moonlight.

Summer ended of course, and as fall approached, George and Chris knew that it meant that school would start again soon, and that they would only get to see each other on weekends because they went to different schools. It was a prospect grim enough to sap the fun out of their last summer days, which, regrettably, would be spent around crowded malls with their parents shopping for clothes and new school supplies.

The two cousins entered the fifth grade and as the weeks wore on, they settled into a predictable routine. Summer receded into a distant memory, and the cousins began to cast their thoughts towards Halloween and the Thanksgiving and Christmas holidays.

"It was late October," George recalls. "I was born on Halloween and Chris… well, he went away just a couple of days before I turned 10. We'd already made plans to go trick-or-treating." George was going to dress up as a bum, as he always did, the sort of low-maintenance costume that appealed to his efficient nature. His cousin had spent weeks planning for a teenage mutant ninja turtle costume, which he had bought with his own allowance money. On the weekend before Halloween, he brought the costume over, dressed himself and then scared George's mother half to death when he sprang from behind a door and yelled, "Cowabunga!"

On Sunday night, George fell asleep, dreading the following school day. He would have to wait until Wednesday for Halloween and his birthday. It was the day on which he got presents from his family and friends *and* candy from perfect strangers! He drifted off to sleep, imagining the mounds of candy he and his cousin would collect in their pillowcases, but he woke up a few hours later with his brow covered with sweat. "I remember waking up to the sounds of someone crying," George says. "I'm not even sure if it was in my dream or not, because I can distinctly remember hearing it in my sleep and after I woke up."

The sobbing was coming from outside his window. George jumped down from his bed and pulled up the window blinds. The streets were bathed in the orange glow of the streetlights and George saw a small figure standing on the sidewalk. The boy was about to cross the street and then vanished before George's eyes. George was stunned—not only had the boy disappeared into nothingness, he resembled his cousin, who must surely have been asleep in his bed just blocks away.

"I didn't think anything of it," George says. "I just put the blinds down and went back to bed. I just told myself I must have imagined it all." George drifted off to sleep once more and began to dream. In his dream, it was day, and looked to be sometime in the late afternoon. Everything looked familiar, and as he stood and looked around him, he realized that he was standing on a street in his neighborhood just a few blocks from his house. Across the street was the same boy he'd seen earlier from his window. The boy, with his back towards George, didn't see him at all. He was just standing there, on the sidewalk, watching a team of other kids kicking around a soccer ball.

One of the players kicked the ball over the boy's head, sending it bouncing into the street. The boy turned to retrieve it for them. From where George was standing, he could see a bus rumbling down the street. George yelled out to warn the boy, but when he opened his mouth, nothing came out. "I can remember trying so hard to get him to hear me and to get his attention," George says. "I was waving my arms, trying to scream. But I couldn't make a sound. It was so strange. I can remember my mouth moving and my tongue trying to make the sounds. But nothing." He was mute.

As George watched, the boy ran into the street, directly into the path of the bus. The bus driver tried to brake, but it was too late. He could hear the screeching of tires skidding along the pavement, and George watched as the boy disappeared beneath the bus. The air was suddenly filled with the acrid scent of burnt rubber. The next thing George could recall, he was waking up in his bed to the sounds of his own screams.

Even then, at almost 10 years of age, George knew that there was something significant about what he had seen. It was so detailed and vivid, but when he spoke to his mother about it at breakfast, she dismissed it as being nothing but a bad dream. He trusted that she knew best. She didn't seem concerned, so why should he? Still, he had her promise that she would call his aunt as soon as she got home from work that night, just to make sure that his cousin was all right.

The school day passed even slower than usual. "I just sat there, in my desk," George says, "watching and watching that clock tick. The end of the day just couldn't come soon enough." When the final bell rang, George quickly packed his things and waited anxiously outside for the school bus. When the bus dropped him off near his home he got off and sprinted home as quickly as he could. Almost immediately, he knew something was wrong.

When he got into the house, everything was eerily quiet. Normally, his mother would be ready at the door to greet him with a snack in hand. The kitchen would be abuzz with activity, with pots on the stove bubbling away and she would be frantically cooking. But that afternoon, the house was still, as if it was inhabited by ghosts and not by the living.

George went through the house, calling out for his mother. Deep down inside of him, he knew that something terrible had happened and he knew that it had something to do with his dream. He walked up the stairs, pausing before every step as if he could somehow affect the past if only he stepped in the right place and breathed in the right way. His parents' bedroom door was slightly ajar, and behind it, he could hear, ever so faintly, his mother sobbing. He felt nauseous as he pushed the door open. She motioned for George to come over and held her arms out as if ready to embrace him.

In halting tones, George's mother told him that his cousin had been killed. He had been run over by a transit bus, just after school had been let out. Chris had been waiting, as he always did, on the curb for his mother to come pick him up. But she had been late that day and as he waited, his attention turned to the soccer practice that was taking place in the field. One of the boys had accidentally kicked the ball over his head. Chris, who was always eager to help out, ran to retrieve the wayward ball. He never saw the bus bearing down upon him, and he was killed instantly. His mother had discovered what had happened when she arrived just a few minutes later.

George listened to his mother, horrified. His dream from the previous night was a premonition, a psychic warning, and he'd been too naïve and clueless to do anything about it. All night, he lay in bed crying and wondering if he could have done something to prevent his cousin's death. When he asked his mother about it, she just hugged him and insisted that he couldn't have done anything at all.

George didn't go out trick-or-treating that year. His cousin's costume went unused. Nor did George celebrate his birthday. It didn't feel right. Even now, almost 15 years after the fact, George still feels guilty on Halloween. "Every birthday I have," he says, "just reminds me that Chris doesn't have one." Every now and then, he'll allow himself to be coaxed out for a small celebration. Most times, though, he'll just shut himself away from the world for the night and wonder about "what if." What if he had acted upon his instincts? What if he had warned Chris or his aunt earlier that day? Every Halloween, the memories of his cousin come flooding back.

2
Strangers Among Us

Mario's Arrival

It's not easy being a psychic. Not only do you have to worry about your field's reputation being sullied by charlatans and fakes out to bilk trusting and unsuspecting people out of their money, you also have to fight against your own clients' expectations to hear only what they want to hear. After all, the truth isn't always what you expect or even believe, and in cases such as those, all Michael J. Kouri can do is sit back, bide his time and wait for events to prove him right.

Kouri is selective when he does a reading; he won't accept just anyone's money. Relying on a personal touch, Kouri travels to clients' homes, whether it is in his home of Pasadena or beyond. Clients have to be worthy of the commute. It's why he refuses to refund fees. Some clients haven't been exactly happy with that policy, at least initially, but they usually come around.

One such client, who runs a gallery in Laguna Beach, California, contacted Kouri for a reading. Before he went, Kouri prepared a list of 300 names and then made the 90-mile drive to her home. He gave her the list of names, which she read over. Many of the names were familiar to her—her mother, her grandmother, her husband, her sister, her hairdresser, the beautician who did her nails and even the cashier at the grocery store. One name, however, caught the client's attention. Mario. She racked her brains, but came up with nothing but blanks. Mario, to the client, simply did not exist.

Kouri warned his client that she might find what he had to say to be preposterous and fantastic, but he proceeded to describe Mario and who he would be in her life. Mario was from Greece. He had gray, curly hair and a scruffy beard with a ragged appearance that belied his wealth. On his pinkie, there was a diamond ring set with a stone of five carats. He was going to shop at the gallery for a half-hour and in that time, spend an exorbitant amount of money. Finally, Kouri revealed that Mario had a yacht and it would be upon this yacht that his client would marry Mario. The client was skeptical, but thanked Kouri for the reading.

The following day, Kouri checked his e-mail and found a nasty message from the gallery owner demanding a refund. She claimed that the reading wasn't worth the money she had spent, but Kouri begged to differ and informed her that no refund would be forthcoming. He had driven a total of 180 miles, given what he considered a "really good reading," reminding her how she had been amazed by what he had said about her family. Kouri never heard from the woman again. Her silence probably had a lot to do with the fact that Kouri blocked her from his inbox. He didn't need that sort of negativity cluttering his life.

Months later, Kouri was back in Laguna Beach visiting some friends. As he walked down the boardwalk, he heard a voice calling out his name and saw a woman running towards him. It was the client from the gallery. She was deliriously happy and Kouri couldn't help but notice that she was wearing a pink diamond ring with a stone that had to be at least eight carats. Kouri, with a knowing smile, asked his former client how her gallery was doing. She breathlessly described how three months after her reading, a man fitting Kouri's description arrived in the gallery. His car had broken down and he needed to call a tow truck. The first thing that the client had noticed about the stranger was his stench and his appearance. The guy looked like a bum.

As he sat at the counter waiting for the tow truck, he began speaking to the client, asking her about the sculptures, earrings and jewelry that she had on display. Within a half hour, the stranger had agreed to buy $10,000 dollars worth of merchandise. He handed her a credit card and, much to her surprise, the electronic transaction was accepted. Every day that week, the man, whose name was Mario, came into the gallery. He had been interested in more than just art. Within months, they were engaged.

The client had tried contacting Kouri repeatedly through e-mail without success to tell him what had happened and to apologize for the way she had treated him. Kouri appreciated the apology but it wasn't necessary. Her happiness was all the satisfaction he needed.

The Touch

Leslie knows that it's called derma-optic perception now—the ability to access information through just a touch. But years ago, when she first realized that she was blessed with this peculiar ability, she was just grateful that it helped warn her about a dangerous situation that involved her young daughter, Jessie.

When Leslie first met Jason (all names have been changed to protect identities), he was in his late teens and, from all appearances, seemed the very picture of responsibility and morality. His family had recently moved to their town of Milan, Ohio, and Jason was a model student who often spent his spare time volunteering to work with the elderly. Even her children seemed to take to him when he came by their house for the first time. He spoke knowledgeably to her eight-year-old son, Carl, about the Transformers and G.I. Joe and kept Jessie in smiles with an assortment of coin tricks. He seemed perfect and, after a succession of unreliable and distracted babysitters who seemed more interested in making a quick buck than caring for her kids, Leslie wasted no time in securing his services.

It seemed, initially, as if her instincts were correct. Her children crowed about Jason, offering glowing and ecstatic reviews. Carl called Jason "the coolest," while Jessie adored that he wasn't too macho to play along with Jessie's My Little Pony dolls. Leslie counted her blessings and considered herself so fortunate to have found the ideal babysitter. Of course, it was only the calm before the storm.

From all appearances, Jason seemed to be the perfect babysitter.

Without warning, Jessie began to protest whenever she was told that Jason was going to come over. She would plead with her mother to find another babysitter, crying that she just didn't like him anymore. Leslie was thoroughly perplexed. She consulted Carl about Jason and found, to her increasing puzzlement, that Carl's opinion of the babysitter stayed the same. He still thought the world of Jason. Trusting the word of her older son, Leslie decided Jessie was still very young and temperamental and could not see anything to suggest that she should be suspicious of Jason.

One evening, Leslie and her husband returned home. They paid Jason and he went merrily along his way. The parents went to bid their children good night. Carl was already asleep, his toys scattered like land mines all over the floor. Jessie was in her bed crying and shaking with her sobs. Leslie sat down beside her and swept her up in her arms. Combing back Jessie's hair, Leslie kissed her daughter on the forehead and asked what was wrong. Jessie refused to say a word. Leslie stayed with her until she stopped crying and drifted off to sleep.

Leslie left the room, making sure to leave the door slightly ajar and to turn the night light on. She went back downstairs to clean up the night's dishes when she noticed that Jason had left his school jacket draped over a kitchen chair. Leslie decided to return it to him the following day. But when she picked the jacket, the strangest thing happened.

In her mind's eye, she saw a scattering of images—children that she had seen at church, Jason, and different homes and different rooms. The images fluttered by so quickly that she had trouble seeing anything, but then the images began to sharpen, and what she saw horrified her. Jason, the model student, the volunteer and varsity athlete, was a predator. He had been abusing the girls that he had been watching. The jacket fell from Leslie's hands and she collapsed into a chair. Now she understood the reason behind Jessie's sudden disdain for Jason. The jacket lay on the floor like a shroud and Leslie stared at it, wondering exactly what had happened. Was she going crazy? Had she just imagined the whole thing? She hesitated as she reached for the jacket. As soon as her hand grazed its red cloth, the images began again. It had been no accident. Somehow, by touching something he had worn, Leslie had been able to see into his life.

She never did return the jacket to Jason. When he came by the following day to retrieve it, she told him never to come to their home again and that she would warn everyone about him. To Jessie, she promised her that she would never let any harm come to her again. When Jessie learned that Jason would no longer be babysitting, she finally broke her silence. She hadn't spoken earlier, fearful of Jason's threats. "If you tell anyone what happened," he had hissed, "something very bad will happen to you." Jessie, just seven and terrified, believed him.

From that time on, any time she interviewed a babysitter, Leslie insisted on hanging up their coats. If her derma-optic perception failed her and she didn't see anything at all, she chose to listen to her children, especially Jessie.

Cash to Go

Most people spend their summers away from college working or, if they're extremely fortunate, do absolutely nothing but bask in the sun, free from fluorescent lights, essays and exams. Jessie, on the other hand, spent her summer of 2000 away from Ames, Iowa, in Des Moines not working, not relaxing, but foiling crime. It was unlike any summer she had anticipated and will forever be remembered for its bizarre occurrences. She still wonders if everything that happened that one August evening was nothing more than a coincidence or if there had been some higher force or power at work. Whatever the cause, Jessie likely saved her life and the lives of those who had been with her that particular evening.

The summer had begun innocently enough. Jessie had returned home after her first year at Iowa State University and was ready for four months of a well-earned rest in her parents' house in Des Moines. After she spent a couple of weeks of doing little else but seeing old friends from high school and catching up, Jessie's father insisted that she be more productive with her time. He cut off her allowance and handed her the classifieds. Jessie found a job working as a waitress at a restaurant where a few of her friends also worked, and it wasn't long before she was working most of her nights at the restaurant.

The months passed quickly, and Jessie used the money she had pocketed in tips for her leisure. She wasn't saving much, but that didn't really matter. For the first time in her life, she was able to do whatever she wanted without

On her way to the lounge, Jessie glanced over at the table in the restaurant.

having to beg for money from her father and without having to justify her spending to him. Most of her money went to the pubs and clubs she frequented. After a long night, she and her friends invariably ended up at the restaurant where she worked, eager to take advantage of free food and free beverages. It was on just such a night when Jessie had her first encounter with psychic phenomena.

From Court Avenue, Jessie and her friends made their way to the restaurant. For some reason, Jessie couldn't explain why, but she thought it would be a bad idea from the moment she got into the car. She ignored the sensation, but the feeling continued to gnaw at her. Whatever she did, she just couldn't shake it.

As they drew closer to the restaurant, the feeling intensified. She felt as if going into the restaurant was something she shouldn't do. She rationalized that nothing ever happened there and blamed her feelings on overly warm beer.

Jessie walked into the restaurant and exchanged greetings and small talk with the hostess before making her way into the lounge. When she entered, she saw a man sitting in a booth along the window. Their eyes met for a brief moment, but it was more than enough for Jessie to see his intentions. As she stood there, it was as if a film was unspooling before her very eyes. She saw the man brandishing a gun. He was attempting to rob the restaurant and its patrons. People screamed and ducked under the tables and banquettes when he flailed his gun in front of them. Before long, he began firing his weapon, shattering glasses and mirrors before a terrified crowd. There were splinters of glass everywhere. With a gasp,

Jessie shook herself free from these images. The man stared at her strangely, sipped on his cola and then went back to his food.

Jessie pulled her friends to her side, telling them that they really needed to leave. When they asked why, she explained quickly that it was late and she just didn't want to inconvenience the staff. They nodded in agreement and made their way back to the car. Jessie told them she'd join them in a few minutes once she said hi to some of the staff. As soon as her friends were gone, she picked up the staff phone, dialled 911 and hurriedly told the operator that their restaurant was being robbed. Then, she found the night manager and told him what was about to happen. He stared at her incredulously and laughed. Jessie sighed, and before heading out, she advised him to duck.

Jessie joined her friends in the car. As they pulled away, they heard the sound of what could only have been gunfire. Though she had foreseen what would happen, Jessie found herself in a state of disbelief. It all seemed so surreal and her friends commented that it was lucky that they had decided to leave. Under her breath, she muttered that it had had nothing to do with luck. As they pulled away, they saw police cruisers speeding towards the restaurant.

When Jessie went to work the next evening, the mood in the restaurant was sombre and subdued. It was understandable, of course, given what had happened. Jessie was relieved to hear that no one had been seriously injured. The would-be robber hadn't even managed to lay his finger on a single bill before policemen bursted into the restaurant, threw him down onto a table and cuffed him.

The manager had stayed until early in the morning answering questions. Naturally, he had a few of his own for Jessie, but alas, she had no answers to give. She said it was just intuition, for lack of a better, saner explanation. The manager was so grateful that he offered to give Jessie the rest of the summer off with pay. She was touched by the offer but in the end, she decided to stay and work. She figured that she might as well work the nights. After all, it seemed that only she had the knack for keeping the place safe.

Golf, Arizona and Sting

Finding love is never easy. Even when you think you've found it, it can fade and wither without warning. There are those who manage to find it and hold on to it, but those exceptions are increasingly rare. For the rest, as Pat Benatar sang, "love is a battlefield" and like any army, you're going to need allies. You could turn to any of the increasingly popular personals web sites, like LavaLife or OkCupid, or you could always head down to your local club and partake in some speed dating. Or, failing those, you could, like Charlotte Davis and her daughter, turn to a psychic.

When Charlotte first consulted Barbara Garcia, she seemed like one of the lucky few who had managed to have it all. She was married and she had a large house in the Hollywood Hills with all the attendant benefits of wealth and status. She was happy, or at least, she thought she was. With her love life seemingly secure and stable, Charlotte quizzed Barbara instead about her career. Barbara addressed those concerns but then went a step further and burst Charlotte's bubble. Charlotte, it seemed, was about to become unlucky in love.

Charlotte pretty much scoffed at everything Barbara had told her. After all, the psychic's predictions seemed outlandish, even ridiculous. With her career, the psychic saw Charlotte hosting her own television program. With her marriage, she saw a divorce, after which Charlotte would meet "a tall, blonde, blue-eyed and well-muscled amateur musician and move to Arizona." Parts of Charlotte were, admittedly, intrigued and slightly alarmed, but Charlotte had no ambitions to be on television and had never even considered leaving the cosmopolitan stylings of Los Angeles for the desert charms of Arizona. She left the reading assured that her friends had recommended a psychic severely short on ability. She was in love, had said "I do and 'till death do us part," and that was the end of that.

But then, it happened. Months later, through a combination of networking and being in the right place at the right time, Charlotte found herself hosting a morning educational program on television. The impossible had just become reality, and though Charlotte was having fun on the program and enjoying her new local celebrity, she couldn't help but think that if Barbara had been right about her career, then was she right about her marriage? Her doubts about the psychic were becoming doubts about her marriage. Her husband's personality had seemed different to her in recent weeks. But Charlotte wasn't quite ready to give up on hope just yet.

She pressed the psychic, hoping for a fortune of a different sort, but the prediction remained, depressingly and drearily, the same. The readings, to Charlotte's growing dismay, had even become more detailed and therefore, more alarming, as Barbara confidently described golfing and sailing dates with the tall and blonde musician. "I don't even know anyone who fits that description," Charlotte protested. "You will," Barbara said.

As the days turned to weeks and the weeks into months, Charlotte was becoming ever more convinced that the psychic might just be right after all. There seemed to be little hope for her marriage. Her husband had turned into a cold and unfeeling stranger, but it had taken her months to realize it. When he spoke, it was to damn with faint praise, offering a compliment he'd undo with his very next breath with a stinging and soul-sapping criticism. His transformation had affected her far more greatly than she had ever suspected. "My self-confidence was dropping," Charlotte says. "And it was a very rough, very dark time in my life." Charlotte began contemplating what months before she'd sworn she never would. "I realized that it wasn't good for me to be with him," she says. "I had to get stronger and grow, and I needed to leave him to do it." She did. Charlotte was single, once more, but confident that the next time, everything would be all right. After all, she had a psychic in her corner now.

Shortly after the divorce, Charlotte met a man through a mutual friend. The man looked exactly as Barbara had predicted. They began to date and, as Barbara had foreseen, often went golfing and sailing. Then, the musician talked about the two of them moving to Arizona together. Charlotte was amazed. Barbara had said she would move to Arizona. She had laughed then, but now was actually seriously considering the idea of living in the Grand Canyon State. After all, she would be moving for love, and that couldn't be a bad thing, could it?

"It's a bad idea," Barbara cautioned. "It's going to end badly." To be sure, love can be a wonderful thing, but Charlotte allowed it to cloud her thinking. She wanted to believe in its power so terribly that she ignored Barbara's advice and moved to Arizona. A year later, the relationship was over. She was more in love with the idea of love than with the musician. Even with a trusted psychic to offer advice, love still proved a tricky minefield to navigate. Racked with the self-doubt and ebbing self-esteem that is often the accompaniment to heartbreak, Charlotte resolved to heed the psychic's advice and became more wary and cautious with her romantic notions. "It was good advice," Charlotte says. Naturally, when Charlotte saw her daughter about to commit the same mistakes in love that she had made, not just once, but twice, she tried to intervene.

At 18, Charlotte's daughter had begun modeling part-time and had been asked to appear in a documentary. She agreed. While working on the film, she met and fell in love with a crew member from Germany. "He was tall and blonde," Charlotte says, "and he looked a lot like Sting. My daughter was completely smitten. He was European, he had the accent. Her head was turned by all of that." Charlotte was suspicious of the man, sensing a darkness about him that clashed with his Teutonic good looks.

When her daughter announced that she and her Sting doppelganger were going to wed, Charlotte protested. Unfortunately, just as Charlotte had ignored Barbara's advice when she moved to Arizona, so too did her daughter ignore her. "I was the mother," Charlotte says wryly, "so I didn't know anything."

"My daughter had only been married for a few months," Charlotte recalls, "and even then, when I spoke to her on the phone, she didn't sound like my daughter. Her voice was slow with no expression. The husband verbally abused her and he might even have hit her once or twice. It's anybody guess what would have happened, but she was definitely getting closer and closer to being suicidal and that was what was scaring me." There was something eerily familiar to Charlotte about the downward trajectory her daughter's marriage had taken. Like mother, like daughter, both were unlucky in love and both had married men who were far less than what they appeared to be. Cue the psychic.

At her mother's urging, the daughter went to see the psychic. She took a ring, or it may have been a watch, from her husband and went for her reading. Barbara took the husband's piece of jewelry and through derma-optic perception, was able to tell the daughter that the marriage had been a mistake. The German was abusive, unfaithful and if she stayed with him, the conclusion could be tragic. "I needed my daughter to see the light," Charlotte says, "and to get away from the guy. Barbara really helped her through that. She was the turning point in helping my daughter realize what she was in." A short time later, she divorced the German. The psychic had done nothing more than confirm the daughter's dark suspicions about her husband, but it was more than enough.

The marriage ended, and today, Charlotte's daughter is happily remarried and living in the Los Angeles area. The psychic approves and had even predicted what the new husband would look like. Charlotte hasn't been as successful. Love remains elusive, but she's happier now and knows that, at the very least, she is blessed with knowing Barbara, a tremendous ally when it comes to matters of the heart.

His Cheating Heart

Andrea first met Dave two years ago. She had been working as a bank teller at a bank in Bloomington, Indiana,
while she worked to finish her degree. It wasn't the most
glamorous of jobs, and it meant that she couldn't go out
and hit the clubs until the wee hours of the morning, but
at least it helped pay the bills. And it also helped that it
was at the bank where she first met Dave.

Andrea was the sort of girl who found it impossible to
be alone. For whatever reason, she just didn't feel whole
without someone that she could call a boyfriend. Maybe it
was insecurity, maybe it was her parents' divorce or maybe
it was something else entirely. Whatever it was, she hadn't
been single for more than a couple of months since she
was 16.

When she took the job at the bank, she had been single
for almost half a year, having ended a three-year relationship. She wasn't happy and admits that part of what had
motivated her to find a job was so she could meet someone.
"I just didn't want to be alone," she says. "I hated not having anywhere to go or anyone to be with on Friday nights."
With the benefit of hindsight, Andrea realized that she had
rushed into things with Dave. She didn't really know him,
and if she had, she may have done things a little differently.
She's grateful, then, for her premonition. Though she can't
explain how it happened or why, it was a dream that saved
Andrea from a possibly catastrophic heartache.

She first saw Dave when he came in to make a withdrawal. Initially, they spoke little, just the formalities. But

his visits to the bank were frequent and soon their awkward banter gave way to easygoing small talk. He'd flirt, she'd flirt and then they'd smile and laugh. So when she ran into him at a small bar on Kirkwood Avenue, her courage fortified with vodka, it was simple enough to make the small but significant leap from flirting to something more.

None of her friends really seemed to like Dave all that much. They all claimed that he was pretty much exactly like her last boyfriend and took to calling him "Peter the Second." Andrea paid them little mind. Her friends were all devoted bachelors who seemed to think of any relationship as a poor substitute for a good night at the bars and one-night stands. She should have listened, but instead fell quickly in love (or was it infatuation?) with Dave.

Weeks passed. They became a couple and celebrated anniversaries of everything: their first kiss, their first date and on and on and on. In no time at all, Andrea was convinced that she had found the man with whom she would spend the rest of her life.

She supposes that she should have seen the signs herself. Dave, for all the attention and devotion he lavished upon her, was far from open with her, often reluctant to speak with any sort of intimacy. "You needed a crowbar to get him to talk about anything," she said. While she talked about their future often, he never seemed to look more than a few days ahead, constantly telling her that he just wanted to take their relationship "one day at a time." It made her uneasy, but perhaps that was just his way. Her friends echoed her suspicions. Some of them went as far to suggest that maybe he was seeing someone else. It disconcerted her, but it wasn't until she had the dream that she was able to understand Dave's silence on matters concerning their burgeoning relationship.

Andrea remembers the dream vividly. In it, a girl approached her. The girl looked vaguely familiar and Andrea felt that maybe she had seen her on campus. It was a large campus and the blonde with rosy cheeks and a bubbly smile could have been anyone on the Bloomington campus. The girl approached Andrea and she recalls asking her who she was, but the girl just looked at her and said eerily, "Why don't you ask your boyfriend that question? Ask him about Melissa."

When Andrea woke the next morning, she couldn't forget the dream. She was compelled to ask Dave about Melissa. She didn't quite know how to bring the question up. What was she going to say to Dave? A girl in my dream told me to ask you about her? It sounded ridiculous. Instead, she decided to be bold and just come right out with it. "Who's Melissa?" she asked. Dave was obviously not prepared for the question. He almost choked on his drink. It wasn't the reaction Andrea had been hoping for. The question struck a nerve and Andrea was beginning to feel like she knew that she was about to get some very bad news. Which, of course, she did.

Dave did know a Melissa, and she was more than just a mere acquaintance. Melissa was, in fact, a girlfriend—another girlfriend. It turned out that Dave hadn't exactly been completely honest about certain aspects of his life. For Andrea, it wasn't exactly a surprise. It merely confirmed everything that she had suspected, but had not allowed herself to even consider as true.

Still, it was devastating news. He had been cheating on her with this girl for months and, interestingly enough, Melissa also suspected that he was seeing someone else. Perhaps she had appeared to Andrea in a dream to force an admission of the truth.

Andrea eventually met Melissa. Well, not exactly. She saw Dave and Melissa together one evening a couple of weeks after she had ended her relationship and while she didn't say a word to either of them, she was certain that the girl was Melissa. After all, she looked exactly like the girl who had appeared to Andrea in her dream.

It was a bizarre time, but Andrea admits that the experience, in the end, was a fortunate one. In the aftermath, as Andrea mulled over what had happened and what she could have done differently, she came to the conclusion that it was better for her to just spend some time on her own. She cheerfully admits that she is single and independent now and is strangely grateful to both Dave and Melissa.

Cabin Fever

For Matthew and Edward, friends from the time they were small children growing up across the street from one another in Boulder, Colorado, their annual hiking and camping trip began in 1994 when they were both 16. Each year, no matter where they were or what they were doing, they always made sure that they returned to Boulder in July to head out for hikes in Rocky Mountain National Park or Mesa Verde or fishing in Black Canyon of the Gunnison. They had a list of hikes and were intent on completing as many of them as they could. For the two friends, their trips were a chance to renew and strengthen their friendship. It was a time that was truly theirs and theirs alone—it was their tradition.

Shaun also had his traditions. An engineer, Shaun found that his work often left him with little time or energy to explore Colorado's ecological wonders in the way he had as a youth. It'd been years since he'd set foot on Mount Ouray or Pikes Peak. But in 1994, Shaun decided it would all change. He had children now and wanted them to experience the wilderness as he had. What he had in mind was an annual family trip away from civilization and to that end, Shaun bought some property and had a cottage built in southern Colorado, near the Pike and San Isabel National Forests. With nothing but verdant stands of pine, spruce and aspen sprawling out in every direction towards snow-capped mountains, Shaun felt that he had finally found his own utopia. He brought his family there for weeks during the summer, losing himself in his rustic

Eden. There, he could forget work and teach his children about the flora and fauna around them. Just as for Matthew and Edward, nature was refuge and ritual for Shaun. In 2001, misfortune and fate would meet, and the three lives would be intertwined forever.

Matthew and Edward had decided that their destination in 2001 would be southern Colorado. They'd never been to the area and felt ready for a little exploration. Their trip began with a couple of simple day hikes, just to get their legs going and the blood flowing. At the end of the first day, with the fresh air coursing through their systems, their senses were alive with their surroundings. The friends settled down into a dinner of freshly caught fish and a couple of beers and spent the rest of the night talking under an impossibly starry sky. Matthew and Edward savored and treasured these moments. They'd just graduated from college, Matthew from the University of Colorado and Edward from Arizona University. With their futures looming, they saw the trip as a last vestige of their rapidly dimming youth, though neither of them acknowledged it at the time. The trip was a welcome sojourn from reality.

Miles away, Shaun and his family were enjoying the night too. As his wife pointed out constellations to their children, Shaun sat on the porch, indulging in an after-dinner smoke from his pipe. He watched as the smoke drifted lazily from his pipe and disappeared into the darkness of the night. With a yawn, he kissed his wife on the cheek and headed into the cabin. They would be leaving tomorrow evening and he wanted to be rested for the drive.

Matthew and Edward woke up early the next morning. They shook the chill from their bones and had a small breakfast of oatmeal and apples. They packed their sacks and set off, ready to conquer the trails. There was a spring in their step and the day was just beginning. They had no idea what lay in store for them.

Shaun spent his last day at his cabin in bliss. He fished along with his son, daughter and wife and was very proud when his son caught his first fish. They walked through the meadows and forests, and Shaun documented their last day with his camera and tripod.

As the day waned and the temperature began to drop, Matthew and Edward were still hiking. They had made good progress, but even the most sure-footed of hikers is not immune to error. Whatever the reason—be it fatigue or carelessness—Edward's footing slipped on the path. He tried vainly to recover his balance, but before he knew it, he was tumbling backwards down a not-so-gentle mountain slope. In his panic, Edward grabbed at anything, but roots only slipped through his fingers, and all he got were cuts from the sharp crags of the rocks below. Matthew watched helplessly as his friend fell. He was aghast when Edward's left leg seemed to flail independently from his body and when Edward's head slapped against a rock with a crack that thundered, or so it seemed to Matthew, through the trees.

After what had seemed like a lifetime, Edward's body drifted to a stop when his pack snagged onto some branches. Matthew could tell that it was bad and that the situation was only going to get worse. He made his way down the slope as quickly as he could, keeping his weight low and back. When he reached Edward, he was relieved to see that his friend was unconscious but breathing. His leg was definitely broken. Miles away from their car on an isolated trail in the dark, Matthew took a breath and wondered exactly what to do.

Further down, Matthew could see that the slope opened into forest and meadow. It seemed easier to take Edward down that way than to try and drag him back up, so Matthew carefully moved him down the slope. He didn't know how severe his Edwards's injuries might be, but he knew that his friend needed help and would need it soon. At the bottom of the slope, he rested to collect his strength. While taking a sip of water, Matthew peered into the encroaching darkness and noticed a light off in the distance. With a steady pace, he estimated that he could probably reach it in under an hour. He wasn't completely comfortable with leaving Edward behind, but he had no choice. The guy was too heavy. Matthew placed his backpack under Edward's head and left a note telling him that he would be back soon. And off he went.

Meanwhile, Shaun and his family finished up their dinner before preparing to leave. He and wife cleaned the cabin and put everything in storage until the next time they visited. They were ready to go two hours later than Shaun had planned, not that he minded. He loved the cabin. He sighed and took one last look at the place before he turned off the lights and locked the door. His minivan moved slowly down the gravel driveway.

Matthew ran hard. He ran until his lungs burned and then he ran some more. He was grateful now for all the time he'd put into running over the last couple of years.

The light was telescoping, growing larger with each step, but then it went out. Matthew groaned and, for the first time, he was starting to get desperate. He stood for an unsteady moment and then continued. Maybe the people who lived there had just gone to sleep. Maybe they hadn't gone out. If they had, he'd just wasted a whole lot of time.

Shaun drove on the dark road before him. The children were engaged with their Game Boys. His wife slept, exhausted. He was tired, too. He took a sip of his thermos of coffee and went back to his driving. His mind drifted to work and the projects he'd blissfully ignored for a couple of weeks. The thoughts caused him to frown slightly. But there was another notion in his head, an idea that was turning and twisting itself into his consciousness. Something was telling him to turn around and not because he wanted to, but because he needed to. The imperative was rising with a propulsive force. Had he forgotten to turn the stove off? Was the cabin unlocked? Something was amiss, but it was far more substantial and grave than the stove or the cabin. He turned his minivan and drove back towards the cabin.

With a gasp, his clothes drenched with sweat, Matthew reached the cabin. He bounded up the steps of the porch and pounded on the window. Pressing his face against the glass, he peered inside, but could see nothing but dim shapes and various shades of black. His heart was pounding and he was gasping with each breath. Cursing, he ran to the front and pounded on the door, while he yelled out hello. There was still no response. Turning, he squinted his eyes as two headlights approached on the gravel road.

Shaun stopped his minivan. There was a guy on his porch, obviously in trouble. He was waving his arms and yelling about someone. Quickly, Matthew explained everything that had happened, and Shaun ran to his cabin and phoned for help. Matthew, luckily, had remembered to record Edward's location from their GPS indicator. The helicopter would find him easily.

Edward had suffered a major concussion and had broken his leg in a number of places. He regained consciousness in the hospital with Matthew by his side. If it wasn't for Shaun's intuition to return to his cabin that evening, Edward could have suffered an even worse fate. The doctors were worried that Edward might have lost full use of the left leg, but he proved them wrong through a rigorous and painful rehabilitation that tested both his body and spirit.

The following year, Edward and Matthew got together again for their trip. Edward's leg hadn't fully healed, but it didn't matter. They returned to southern Colorado, to spend a week with Shaun and his family. It became their new summer tradition—to enjoy life and nature with their new friends.

Bringing Up Baby

Neal doesn't exactly know how to classify his experiences. He doesn't know if it's a ghost story or if it was a psychic experience. All he knows is that his baby's life was saved and he's still not exactly sure how.

Neal's story takes place just a couple of years ago, in the Texas town of Amarillo. Neal had been born and raised in Amarillo, but had left long ago for the big city glamor of Houston. Neal had planned a trip to Amarillo for his parents to meet his wife and new son for the first time. The trip was supposed to be a joyous occasion, but in an unfortunate coincidence, he was also returning to his small, dusty hometown to attend the funeral of an old friend.

On the day of the funeral, Neal left his six-month-old son with his parents and headed to the cemetery. Once the sombre affair was all over, Neal and his wife began wandering among the tombstones after everyone else had left. Intrigued by the age of the cemetery, they checked the tombstones for the names and dates of the deceased. They hadn't been walking long when they noticed an old, hunched woman walking down the street that ran parallel to the cemetery grounds.

She had an odd gait about her and she limped along the pavement slowly. Despite her hunch, she appeared quite tall. She was dressed entirely in black clothing that looked like a costume from the early 1920s. Neal's wife muttered that the old lady must shop for clothing at a vintage store. Her clothing was the least of Neal's concerns—after all, she was an old woman so it wasn't at all unusual

Neal and his wife wandered to look at the tombstones in the cemetery, but something else caught their attention.

that she would be wearing old clothing—but there was something else about her that caught his attention. He couldn't quite explain what or why, but he felt that something was wrong, that there was something different about the woman.

She was not more than 20 feet from Neal and his wife when she suddenly stopped and turned to face the couple. She stared at Neal, knowingly. It was almost as if she recognized him. Her craggy face looked at him with a sweet smile. She nodded, turned and began to walk away. His wife pulled on his arm. Neal turned to her and she stared at him perplexed. "Do you know her?" she asked. Neal shook his head and looked for the old woman, but she was gone. The old woman had vanished. It was as if she had never been there.

The visit to the cemetery was over. Neal grabbed his wife by the arm and hurried her towards their rental car. She walked awkwardly because her entire body was stiff with shock. They drove back to his parents' house in silence, unsure of what to say or what to think. Neal still had the aching sense of dread that something terrible was about to happen. Neal and his wife finally spoke about the old woman later that night, as they lay in bed, each desperately trying to reassure the other that what they had seen had not been some sort of hallucination.

They stayed in Amarillo for a couple more days, allowing Neal's wife to get acquainted with her in-laws and for his parents to fawn and coo over their grandchild. But a feeling of impending doom had haunted Neal since he'd seen the old woman.

When their six-month-old son fell gravely ill with a fever, Neal and his wife decided to cut their trip to Amarillo short. They were frantic to get their son back to his pediatrician in Houston. They packed quickly and boarded the next available train home. When their son's condition steadily worsened, they became so panicked that they began combing the passengers of the train for a doctor. They managed to find one who agreed to take a look at their son. His diagnosis was grim. Their son's temperature was over 100 degrees and he did not know what he could do for the child. Death was very possible.

Neal and his wife clutched their child, trying to ignore the sounds of his labored breaths. They prayed for some sort of divine intervention to save their child's life. As Neal sat there with his silent prayers, he felt peculiar, as if someone was watching him. Out of the corner of his eye, he noticed that someone was standing beside him. He looked up and was stunned to see the old woman that they had seen outside the cemetery, just days earlier. She greeted him with the same sweet little smile, but this time, Neal noticed the sadness and regret that permeated her gaze.

"I see your baby is very ill," she whispered in a surprisingly soothing voice. She knelt down, took off her gloves and placed one wrinkled hand upon the baby's forehead. With closed eyes, her hand rested on the child's head for a moment. Then she stood up and pulled her long black gloves back on. "Your baby will be fine," she said, "I just took him to see my doctor." With a rustle of her long, dark dress, the old woman vanished.

Neal and his wife, still clutching their small son, couldn't bring themselves to speak. They both felt that the moment had been sublime and ethereal—to speak would have displaced it all. "I know it sounds crazy," Neal admits, "but when the old woman touched my son, I just knew that he would be all right. I never doubted it for a second."

Within half an hour, their son's fever had broken. Two hours later, he was cooing and breathing normally. By evening, their son was smiling once again, lighting up their home with his infectious grin.

To this day, Neal has no idea who the old woman was. He's certain that she was not of this physical world and that she had come to prepare him for his son's illness and, in the end, she saved his son's life. He's got no idea how to thank her, though he presumes that she probably knows how grateful he is.

3
Help Is On The Way

Car Crash

Richard treats every day as a gift. It's an attitude he's adopted in the wake of an experience that's left him with a greater thirst for life and a stoked curiosity about psychic phenomena.

Growing up, Richard says that he had no interest whatsoever in paranormal or psychic phenomena. Sure, he read ghost stories and, like most children, found them frightening and fascinating, but it was a fondness that was quickly displaced with school, sports and girls, though not necessarily in that order. When he finished school, it was all about money and his career. He had dismissed psychic phenomena as nothing but fiction, so it was quite a shock when he had a vision three years ago. It was even more damning to Richard's scepticism when he realized the vision probably saved his life.

It all happened on a sunny day in Palm Beach, Florida in the summer of 2001. Richard was having dinner at his aunt's. A stock trader by day, Richard didn't have much time for home-cooked meals and gladly accepted his aunt's invitation. When he got there, he suddenly remembered why he didn't visit his aunt often. She was a recent immigrant to the country, having arrived just a few years before from Japan. Her English was poor and Richard's Japanese was poorer, so their conversations were simply awkward. She usually spoke to him as if he were three years old, asking about whether he had a girlfriend or recounting embarrassing stories from his youth.

When dinner was served, Richard gratefully accepted a bowl and began to eat quickly. Richard knew that the sooner he finished eating, the sooner he could leave. Satisfied, and after washing the dishes, Richard was at the door putting on his shoes as his aunt looked on. He was about to kiss her goodbye when he saw images flash though his mind.

He saw his car collide with another car. The other car was moving in reverse without, it seemed, any regard for Richard's car directly behind it. It gathered speed before coming to a complete halt with a jarring crash. Richard's windshield imploded with a loud crack. Shards of glass sprayed in all directions. Richard was horrified. He bid his aunt a hasty farewell so he could move the car before it would be hit.

As he turned to open the door, his aunt grabbed his arm and in her broken English, simply said, "You must wait. Wait. Wait." Richard tried to pull away, but his aunt's grip was strong and unyielding. Once more, she said, "Wait."

There was authority in her voice, a previously unknown inflection that gave Richard pause. He relented and stopped resisting his aunt's pull. Instead, he just stood there and looked out at his car through the window. His aunt grasped his arm and told him to watch. And so he did.

He watched and before his eyes, his vision unfolded. A car slammed, in reverse, into his car and rocketed down the street. Richard's windshield had shattered. The driver and passengers seats were covered in glass shards. Glass was scattered along the back seat as well. It became very clear why his aunt wanted him to stay.

In an instant, the windshield imploded from the impact, and shards of glass were everywhere!

If he had gone out to move his car as he had originally intended, he would have been sitting in the car exactly when his windshield was smashed. The glass shards would no doubt have brought serious harm. He stared at his aunt and she just smiled and said, "Now you can go."

As it turned out, not only did Richard have a vision, so did his aunt. Hers, however, was just a little different. She saw the same accident, only she saw Richard in his car when the other car crashed into him. The impact shattered the windshield and trapped Richard inside. When she saw him lying in his front seat bleeding heavily from his wounds, she knew that she had to protect her nephew from imminent danger.

When Richard heard his aunt's account, he sat in shock, floored by the confluence of events. When he had his vision, he wasn't worried about his life. He was concerned with the damage to his car and the hassle of dealing with his automobile insurance company. It never occurred to him that he might be placing himself in harm's way. Looking back, he was much happier with the broken windshield, shattered fender and damaged headlights than he thought he would have ever been. Richard has meals with his aunt far more often now, and though they still have awkward conversations, he realizes how important his aunt is to him.

9/11

Ever since he was a teenager, Michael J. Kouri has been keenly aware of his abilities and gifts. When he was 16, Kouri had his first paranormal experience, interacting openly and easily with the ghost of a woman. From that time, Kouri has honed and developed his abilities, and though people who read with him or watch him work are often amazed, Kouri doesn't consider what he does as anything special. He believes that every individual has these abilities, but unlike the majority of the population, he had never been conditioned to dismiss his psychic gifts. Kouri credits his mother and father, both highly creative individuals, for "encouraging [him] to be who [he] wanted to be." He was never taught to "not trust himself, to hate himself and to hate others."

Kouri is a man of many trades. Though he calls himself a professional "psychic, medium and parapsychological investigator," Kouri sings, plays the piano and appraises antiques as well. What makes him even more remarkable is that, for more than 25 years, Kouri has investigated over 8000 haunted sites, conducted countless "communication circles" (more commonly known as séances, which he thinks has been tainted by its less-than-holy associations) and given many more readings. Kouri speaks so passionately about his work that even the most skeptical people would be hard-pressed to hold on to their disbelief. When he says that he "loves to help people" and that he still gets "so excited when he gets a direct hit," you want to believe him. His enthusiasm is infectious.

Still, Kouri admits that being a psychic and medium can take its toll. With so much information coming at him in waves, some of it extremely personal and private, Kouri can find it all overwhelming. He does his best to filter and analyze the information and then move on. There are those times, though, where he can't forget and he, like many of his clients, stands in awe.

In the summer of 2001, Kouri took a trip to New York City to be a guest on the television show, *The View*. After the show, Kouri made his way to Sleepy Hollow, New York, where he had been asked to perform an impromptu investigation of co-host Meredith Vieira's house. He also led a communication circle, during which he went into a trance for four hours and offered premonitions of the future. Many predictions were made, but the one most notable was Kouri's belief that "a major disaster is going to happen in New York City." He admits that he didn't know what it was going to be or where it was going to be, but when he made the prediction, Kouri's body was shaking and the flame on a candle in the middle of the dining room table rose 12 inches into the air. "Everyone was floored," Kouri says, "absolutely floored." Kouri, through a spectacular coincidence that the medium calls a "subconscious premonition," narrowly avoided being one of the victims of the 9/11 terrorist attacks in New York City.

In September 2001, Kouri was back doing work on the news program, *20/20*. He was scheduled to fly back to California on the 11th, in the morning. But while he was in New York, Kouri felt something compelling him to check his answering machine. "I usually never check my answering machine when traveling. I just check my messages when I get back," Kouri says. "But this time, a voice inside told me to check it." He did and found a message asking him to give a lecture in Orange County, California, on the 12th. Kouri had originally committed to the event, but it had been canceled just before he'd left. In his absence, it seemed as if organizers had pulled together enough money to secure Kouri's services.

Kouri decided to change his schedule and return to California earlier than he had planned to give himself time to prepare for his lecture. He flew out on the 10th. A day later, Kouri, like the rest of the nation, woke to the devastating news that four planes had been hijacked. Two had been flown into the World Trade Center. Another crashed into the Pentagon. And another had crashed in a wooded area in Pennsylvania. Kouri watched the news in horror. Originally, Kouri had planned to make his way down to Salem, Massachusetts, to visit a friend and investigate sites associated with the Salem Witch Trials. He had been scheduled to return to Los Angeles from Boston on United Airlines Flight 175 on the morning of September 11th, the very same flight that crashed into the south tower of the World Trade Center a little after 9:00 AM. If Kouri hadn't checked his answering machine two days earlier, he would have been killed. Kouri credits his spirit guides with saving his life, proof that even psychics need a little guidance every now and then.

Like many other Americans, Kouri tried to put 9/11 behind him. But it continued to rear its head in small, unusual ways that underscored the day's horror.

In October 2003, Kouri was to give a lecture at the Egyptian Theater in Hollywood, and even though he was the night's entertainment, he had trouble gaining entry to the building. A big, burly volunteer with bright red hair was working the door and blocked Kouri's way. He kept asking for Kouri's ticket, but Kouri didn't have one. After 20 minutes of haggling with the volunteer, he radioed the organizer, who finally cleared the matter up. Kouri noticed that the man with the red hair had a fiery aura and decided that he was obviously very stressed.

During the lecture, Kouri saw the same man sitting in the audience. He was easy to spot because his aura looked like flames. Kouri felt his spirit guides were guiding him towards the volunteer, but after the tussle at the door, Kouri really didn't feel like dealing with him. He ignored the voices, but then, the volunteer raised his hand. "I guess I had to go there," Kouri says, "I wasn't really in control. The spirit guides were."

The man apologized for what had happened earlier. Kouri enlightened the ignorant audience, which laughed when they heard Kouri's account. To the man, he said, "I saw your aura earlier when you were upset and it was red. I saw flames, smoke and fire around you, as if you'd been involved in a horrific accident. You were involved in a fire. Were you a fireman?" The man nodded and explained that he was the only fireman from his battalion to survive the collapse of the World Trade Center. In the aftermath, his wife, fearful of what might happen if he continued to work as a fireman, convinced him to retire and move to California. The audience was aghast and remained hushed at his revelation.

Kouri, perhaps sensing the need to relieve the tension of the crowd, looked at the wife. "You're pregnant," he said. The woman nodded and then proceeded to chastise Kouri. She had planned on telling her husband about her pregnancy the next day, on their anniversary. Kouri had inadvertently ruined the surprise, but it was moments like these that made Kouri grateful for his gift. He may have to suffer visions of earthquakes, hurricanes, floods and other disasters, but for Kouri, it's a small price to pay for bringing joy into a world starving for it.

Brotherly Love

The memory still haunts Edgar Thompson (names have been altered to protect idenitities). And try as he might, he still can't exorcise the vision from his mind. It stalks him and there are still nights when he finds himself staring into the darkness. But restless nights and a haunted soul are more than a fair price to pay for his twin brother's life. He never lets himself think about what might have happened if he'd ignored the premonition.

Edgar has always been close to his twin brother, and one supposes that you can't help but be close with someone with whom you've shared a womb for nine months.

"Our mother was always very strict," recalls Edgar. "I can remember long summers months where my brother was the only person I had to play with. Our mother wouldn't let us out because she was worried about skin cancer and wouldn't let our friends come over because they might make a mess of the house. It was just the two of us, always." In high school, few of their friends ever referred to them by name. They were known simply as the twins. "What're the twins doing tonight?" friends would ask. "Give the twins a call," they would say.

"It was funny," Edgar says, with the trace of a laugh. "Sometimes I even wondered whether or not they even knew our names." As close as Edgar and Allen are, he admits that he was tired of being part of a duo. He longed for his own friends and his own identity by the time high school came to an end. He applied to a number of universities that would take him out of Prince George, British

Columbia, and so intent was he on leaving the province that he never even considered applying to the University of British Columbia.

Allen also wished to leave his hometown and to be known as just Allen Thompson, not Allen Thompson, the twin. His parents, on the other hand, had different ideas. While they were eager for their children to go abroad and have new experiences, they weren't comfortable with the idea of the twins' separation.

As close as the twins were in appearance, they couldn't have been more different in temperament. Edgar was the responsible one, grounded, reasonable and a little shy. Allen was the dreamer, a little impractical, impulsive and outgoing to a fault. Their parents didn't worry at all about Edgar. He had plans for the future and knew exactly what he needed to do to make them happen. Allen, however, seemed content to float along aimlessly with no plans. His parents wanted Edgar to be his anchor.

"Allen really didn't want to go to Queen's, which is where I wanted to go," Edgar recalls, his voice breaking a little at the recollection. "He wanted to go to UBC, to go to the big city, and well, I remember thinking that I didn't really care where he went. I guess I'd have to admit that part of me didn't want him coming to Queen's. Though after everything that happened, I'm eternally grateful that he did. If he hadn't…" Edgar stopped speaking. To go on would be to contemplate what might have happened, and he never lets himself do that.

Allen protested when his parents told him that he would be going to whichever school his twin brother chose. He hated the idea of going to yet another small town and in his mind, they didn't get much smaller than Kingston. But what choice did he have? He wasn't working and didn't have money for tuition, and they certainly wouldn't pay for another school. Reluctantly, he applied to the school, hoping that he would be rejected. When he learned that he had been accepted, he hid the acceptance letter in a drawer in his desk and only told his parents about it weeks later. In the fall of 1992, Edgar and Allen left Prince George and began their new life in Kingston. They had no idea of what lay in store for them there.

Initially, Allen was unhappy, but he had a natural buoyancy about him and he took to campus life quickly. Long nights were spent in blissful inebriation and he luxuriated in the liberation from his strict parents. Having requested separate dorm rooms, Edgar and Allen finally found the lives they had craved for so long. The friends they made were their friends alone and the fact that they were twins was only coincidental, a point of interest rather than the definition of their beings. Indeed, the brothers began seeing less and less of one another. They were in different faculties and they didn't seem to need time for family anymore.

Three years passed and the strangest thing happened. "I missed him," Edgar says. "We were living in the same city and I missed him. How funny is that? Isn't that bizarre? There were times where I would pass him on Princess Street and all we did was exchange hellos. He was becoming a stranger and I didn't like it." Allen admitted as much to his brother one night at a pub. They had come to Kingston to get away from one another, but instead, found themselves drawing closer together.

"I think that we were learning to see each other as individuals," Edgar says. "I realized that while we had always been close, we had only been close because we were twins. But now, we were becoming friends and being twins had nothing to do with it at all."

Of course, being twins may have had something to do with what happened to Edgar and Allen in their final year at Queen's. Being twins, Edgar and Allen had always been asked whether or not they had a psychic connection, as some twins are believed to have. The two always scoffed at such notions.

"Yeah, I was tired of the question," Edgar says with a sigh. "But ask me now, and I'll tell you that I firmly believe in it. How could I not?"

On February 26, 1996, the brothers' beliefs would be altered forever. The day began innocuously enough. It was another dreary winter in Kingston; slush and ice covered the streets and sidewalks, and the limestone campus buildings were nearly indistinguishable from the snow. Allen was still sleeping at his house on University Avenue when Edgar trudged out of his house on Barrie Street to go to his morning lecture. Allen rose a little while later to get ready for his class. He smoked a cigarette, read the paper, did the crossword and then headed off to the bathroom to take a shower.

Edgar was sitting in his class, squirming uncomfortably in his seat as his professor droned on endlessly about public policy. His mind was wandering, and he could barely keep his eyes open to take notes. And then, it happened. Edgar sat up with a start.

"I don't know how to explain it," he says. "But I saw my brother in my head. And he was in pain, and it was as if I could sense his pain, but not really feel it. I could see he had a sudden, blistering headache. I could feel that he was dizzy and nauseous, that he couldn't really see anything. He was in the shower with the water running and then suddenly, he fell. He just collapsed."

Edgar ran from his desk to a pay phone. "I don't know why I acted on it. But I just knew that something had happened to him. I didn't know what but I knew he needed help," he says. He called an ambulance and then proceeded to run to Allen's house. The front door was unlocked, as it always was, and he ran up the stairs to the bathroom. He found Allen slumped against the shower wall with water still running over him. He was unconscious.

Edgar would later learn that his twin had suffered a cerebral aneurysm. Allen had been alone in the house; all his housemates had gone to class and wouldn't have returned until much later in the afternoon. If the paramedics hadn't reached Allen when they did, he would have died from a hemorrhagic stroke.

"I don't know what happened that day," Edgar says, his voice breaking. "But every day, I'm so grateful that it did. Whatever happened saved my brother's life."

Allen didn't escape completely unscathed. He suffered a left-brain stroke, which left him paralyzed on the right side of his body. His speech is slurred, but he is alive. His rehabilitation was long and difficult, but with the help of his family and friends, Allen persevered.

"He's still with us," Edgar says. "And that's all that matters." The twins are now closer than ever. They live in the same city, just blocks away from one another, and speak almost daily. "We have our own lives still," Edgar says, "but I've never been happier to be a twin."

Love Connection

John and Tara first met in their freshman year of high school in the early 1990s. From the start, both knew that there was something different and unique about their relationship. Both of them find it hard to put into words, but it was as if there was an immediate connection between them that made conversations easy and comfortable.

Tara had noticed John on the first day of school, but John, busy with sports and friends he hadn't seen in all summer, didn't. They met through mutual friends one day during lunch hour and the chemistry was immediate. John admits that he had been a bit shallow when he first met her. John liked stunningly beautiful girls who turned heads and sent guys whispering about them. Tara had a subtle prettiness that grew over time. In the first year, their relationship never went beyond scattered conversations during a lunch hour or after school.

At the beginning of their sophomore year, John realized, with a burgeoning of his heart that took him by surprise, that Tara was in a number of his classes. And, for some reason, when she chastised him for not calling her over the summer, he couldn't keep from smiling. John felt the first stirrings of attraction and resolved that this year, he would do something about it. They began to call each other, and interestingly enough, they always called each other when they needed each other most.

Both of them came from broken homes in which their fathers were continually absent and showed little interest in fostering a meaningful relationship. They both tried to show no outward signs of distress or misery, but some days, it wasn't so easy. On those days, Tara would call John. "You need someone to talk with tonight, don't you?" she would ask. John wondered how she always knew when he needed her most. Sometimes, it was John who would call Tara just because he sensed she was sad and miserable. Often, they finished each other's sentences, or knew exactly what the other was thinking without having to hear a word. Their minds were in complete synchronicity.

Tara and John dated for the next two years. But for all their chemistry, their devotion and love, the relationship didn't last. After high school, they parted ways. John was going to college in the east while Tara stayed in the southwest. They spoke often during the first couple of months, but eventually, time apart and distance took their toll. By the time the two of them had graduated, they barely spoke except on the odd occasion when they ran into each other at the local mall in their hometown at Christmas.

It all changed, however, on one peculiar winter's day. John was now living in Massachusetts in a town near Boston. As the snow fell, John sat in an armchair by his window, reading a novel. As he read, his mind drifted, and John began to wonder about Tara. And then, the strangest thing happened. He felt something that pricked his consciousness. Tara was in pain. In his mind's eye, he could see her, battered and bruised. He felt claustrophobic and trapped, and knew that these were not his emotions, but Tara's. Why or how he knew, John could not say, but Tara needed his help. She was in an abusive relationship from which she saw no escape. Compulsion forced him to act.

John needed more than just a phone call to assure him that Tara was okay.

With a prayer, he called Tara's parents, hoping that they hadn't moved or changed their phone number. The phone rang once, twice, thrice. On the fourth ring, a familiar voice answered. Tara's mother was thrilled to hear from him, so it was a simple thing for him to ask for Tara's number and address.

John jotted down her information, surprised to see that Tara was actually living in Connecticut and had been for the last three years. Tara's mother thought that it would be wonderful if he went to see her, and John told her that he intended to. He hung up the phone, wondering if he was crazy. Was he really going to go see her because of a feeling he had? And because he believed that she was in trouble? Was he being melodramatic? John didn't know, deciding to wait a day to see how he felt about it all in the morning.

After a long sleepless night, John woke up the next morning harried and exhausted. The feeling that Tara needed his help had not abated. If anything, John had only become more certain. He picked up the phone, ready to dial her number, but then changed his mind. The situation required more direct action than just a phone call. He looked at a map and calculated that he could be at Tara's house in hours. He jumped in the car and was on his way.

John arrived at Tara's house. With a deep breath, he ambled up its cobblestone walk and rang the doorbell. He was more nervous than he thought he would be, suddenly pondering what exactly he would say. Where would he begin?

John knew instantly that his instincts were right when Tara opened the door. She had tried to cover her bruises with foundation but they were faintly visible. "You never did look good with makeup," he said. Tara smiled before opening her arms to embrace John.

His appearance on her doorstep wasn't a surprise. Somehow, she knew that he would be coming. She was far from happy. Her boyfriend was indeed abusive and she just didn't know how to leave him. Confused and lost, she looked back over her life. She remembered her father, the way he had abused her, both physically and verbally, and how she had confided in John about it. It was his sympathy, his capacity to listen that she needed most and it was during this dark time of her life that she turned to him again.

Tara had actually called John's family the week before, trying to find out where he was, but hadn't been able to phone him. She just didn't feel right about phoning him, so for a week, she had kept his phone number jotted down on a scrap of paper and hoped that maybe John, like always, would sense her distress. He had.

The two spoke for hours that afternoon. John had almost forgotten how wonderful it was to speak with Tara. But there was sadness to it all too. Tara spoke openly, wanting John to excise her pain and to be her comfort. It was a difficult task. John could see the conflict within her. She was confused and didn't know whether to leave or to stay. He did the best he could, hoping that Tara would do the right thing. With his hands in hers, he said goodbye, admitting that he had to head home. He promised to call.

When he called after a week, John was relieved to hear a happier Tara. He noticed that some of her effervescence had returned. She had found her strength and decided, at long last, to shed her abusive boyfriend.

John's visit rekindled their friendship. When Tara came for a visit months later, John asked her to stay. She did. And they've been together ever since.

Automatic Driving

Carl has never had an accident driving. The cynic might scoff and laugh and say that Carl probably doesn't drive. Carl does drive, even though he himself wonders why— New York City isn't exactly automobile-friendly. He has a spotless driving record, but he takes none of the credit. His perfection on the road is the direct result of ESP. Voices in his head guide his hand and it's his psychic ability that has helped him to avert disaster.

Carl will admit that he's had a speeding ticket or two, and like a lot of drivers in New York City, more than a few parking tickets. It seems as if his extra-sensory perception only delivers a warning if he and his vehicle are in imminent danger. The first time it happened, Carl just dismissed it as an example of good fortune. But after the second and third time, he realized, with a shudder of fear, that perhaps there was something else at work. He asked that his real name not be used because he doesn't know how many people would accept his version of the mysterious events.

The first time it happened, Carl was driving from Brooklyn to his office in midtown Manhattan. He had pulled into a left-turning lane and was sitting impatiently, waiting for the green arrow to start flashing. It did and Carl moved his foot, ready to accelerate into his turn. But then, he stopped. It was as if his control of his foot had been usurped by his subconscious— something in his head told him not to go. He sat there as cars behind him began honking their horns in protest. But he refused to move, and it was fortunate that he didn't. Just then, a minivan sped through the intersection from his left, running the red light. The entire incident hadn't taken more than a few seconds, but for a moment, it was if time stood still for Carl. He remembered every single little detail— the song that was playing on his radio, the make and model of the car that was honking behind him, the face of the minivan driver as she had sped by with a vanload of children. The entire episode was shocking. If he had turned left as he had intended, the minivan would surely have plowed into his automobile. He would certainly have been injured, if not killed. Carl was jolted back into reality by the incessant honking of the cars behind him, and he continued, stunned, on his way to work.

Carl never thought about the incident until a couple of months later when he was driving down a street in his neighborhood of Bay Ridge. He pulled up behind a large van and watched it absentmindedly, waiting for traffic to clear so that he could pull around it. He had been thinking about what to buy his girlfriend for her birthday, and then, for no reason, he suddenly felt compelled to back the car up. The thought was so forceful that Carl immediately reversed his car and moved it back several feet. No sooner had he stopped, than the large van in front of him reversed as well. It began hurtling backwards at him and Carl was forced to retreat even farther. In anger, he hammered his car horn loudly, and it was only then that the van stopped. Again, if it hadn't been for the voice in his head, Carl would have been front-ended by a van whose driver had not bothered to check his rear view mirror. As he sat in his car, Carl wondered what exactly had happened. He recalled the incident from months

Without his keen senses, Carl's daily commute from Brooklyn to Manhattan would be hazardous.

earlier and was certain that the two events had to be related. He wondered if he had a guardian angel. Was he blessed with an extra-sensitive intuition? Were the two events completely unrelated? Carl just didn't know.

The last time it happened was only a few months ago when Carl was visiting a friend in Boston. While trying to make sense of the city's network of labyrinth-like roads with its unexpected one-ways and narrow passages, he drove down a small road with just enough room for parking on one side and traffic on the other. The narrow street was making Carl a little nervous.

Coming up on his left, Carl noticed an auto body shop. As he approached it, he had the impulse to brake his car, even though there was no obvious reason to do so. He slammed on his brakes and brought the car to a screeching halt, leaving the acrid scent of burnt rubber in the air. Pedestrians walking the street stopped and turned, wondering what he was doing. Carl sat there with his hands gripping his steering wheel tightly, wondering if he had finally gone crazy. What was he doing?

He eased his foot off the brake to the accelerator when he saw a police cruiser backing out quickly from the garage. He estimates that the cruiser came to a halt just inches or so from his car. Again, if he hadn't done what the voices in his head had told him do, he would surely have been t-boned by the cruiser. (The irony that it happened in front of an auto body shop wasn't lost on him.) The police officer sped off unaware that he missed colliding with Carl's car by just inches.

Carl, as one might expect, looks back on what he calls his psychic experiences with bewilderment. To be sure, he's grateful that there seems to be some paranormal force out there that's intent on keeping him safe while driving, but at the same time, it's called into question his whole belief system and left him with far more questions than answers. Still, he doesn't complain too much because at least he knows that he'll be safe. In the meantime, he continues to drive, ever wary of the voices in his head.

How to Climb A Ladder

Ariana Jacobs never had any intentions of visiting a psychic. Not only was she skeptical about psychic abilities, but she already had a mother who seemed to know everything that was going to happen and, to say the least, it drove her more than a little crazy. She needed guidance, but Ariana had no idea to whom she might turn.

It was the late 1970s and Ariana was wondering who could possibly help her sort out what she saw as a messy and confusing life. "I was a 28-year-old," Ariana says, "with the mentality of an 18-year-old." She wasn't even in her 30s yet and she'd already had two failed marriages, a child and another marriage to an older man on the way. Then, while reading the newspaper one morning, she came across an article that she found especially interesting. It detailed Barbara Garcia and her involvement in the case of the Hillside Strangler. Working as a psychic artist, Barbara had drawn a sketch of what the Hillside Strangler might look like. Ariana remembers thinking, "Wow, that's pretty cool," and left it at that.

A few years later, Ariana heard the psychic artist's name again. "My employer was quite familiar with her," she writes, "and the two owners used her for investment counseling and consultations for their business. One afternoon, her boss told them about his reading with Barbara. He told his employees how she had told him that he would meet a beautiful brunette who would approach him at a business lunch and that before the year was out, they would be married. The reading was treated with some incredulity. Ariana's boss, after all, had spent the better part of two decades with another woman and it seemed obvious to everyone that he never had any intention of giving up his bachelorhood. Ariana laughed and said to her friends upon hearing the prediction, "If that happens, I'll be there to see Barbara within 15 minutes."

Two weeks later, to Ariana's great surprise, her boss returned from a business lunch in Newport Beach beaming with an incredible story to tell. With great excitement, the boss described how a beautiful brunette approached him and told him that she heard of his work and had wanted to meet him to discuss business. The meeting led to romance, and it was clear that her boss was now smitten. The couple wed less than a year later, the psychic's prediction had come true and Ariana was awed. Barbara had helped her boss find love, so Ariana wondered if Barbara could do the same for her. She asked for Barbara's phone number and made an appointment.

Before her appointment, Ariana was asked to come up with a list of 15 questions that she wanted answered. Her mother told her not to wear jewelry and not to tell Barbara anything during the meeting, to "just keep [her] mouth closed and listen." Ariana arrived for her meeting, a little nervous and still somewhat skeptical. "Within two seconds," Ariana says, "Barbara blew me away." Barbara asked Ariana if she had been married. Ariana nodded. Barbara then asked, "Once?" Again, Ariana nodded. Barbara smiled and said, "Let's start this off right. You've been married twice. The first was very short, but we still should count it." Ariana was sold. Her first marriage had been brief, lasting just three months before it was annulled. "How could she ever have known that?" Ariana says, her voice still pitched with amazement.

The pair spoke at length, with Barbara taking notes the entire time. When Barbara was finished and Ariana had a chance to look at what Barbara had written, she realized that Barbara had addressed each of her 15 questions without Ariana having asked one of them. The notes formed a template for Ariana's life with detailed premonitions and warnings that all came to pass as the years went by. Ariana says that after all this time, Barbara has taught her how to "climb life's ladder."

The First Rung: The Child

One of Ariana's questions concerned her two-year-old son. What did his life hold? What would happen with him? Was she leading him along on the right path? Ariana, at the first meeting, had shown Barbara a photograph of her son. "She looked at the picture," Ariana writes, "and told me that he would grow up to be a very important individual. She told me that he was an old soul and that around the second or third grade, the school was going to come to me and tell me that he should be held back a year." She predicted that he would have problems with little things like the tying of his shoelaces and writing numbers, but cautioned that these small deficiencies shouldn't blind Ariana to the fact that her son was brilliant.

Ariana had already noticed that there was something special about her child. He had started speaking extremely early, almost in complete sentences. "At two," Ariana recalls, "Josh was telling me what we should and shouldn't do. He was basically raising me." It seemed incomprehensible that there would be something wrong with him, but Barbara was firm. "When they come to you," she said, "and tell you that they want him to repeat a year, remember what I've told you and say no. Another woman will approach you from the school. Do what she tells you to do."

Her son's verbal skills continued to grow and by the time he was five, he already knew exactly what he wanted from his life and how he was going to get it, and he never hesitated to tell everyone around him. It was a busy time and Ariana admitted that she had forgotten about Barbara's predictions, especially regarding her son.

When Josh's second grade school year came to an end, Ariana was called to the school. At a meeting, she learned that the school believed Josh wasn't ready for the increased work of the third grade and wanted him to repeat the second grade. "When they told me that," Ariana says, "my memory was triggered instantly. It was a déjà vu." As Barbara had told her to do, Ariana said no. She left the school shaken, and on her way to her car, another teacher stopped her. She explained to Ariana that her son was smarter than the school was giving him credit for and that a place called Smarts 4 U would be able to help him.

Smarts 4 U tested Josh and found that he suffered from dyslexia and dysgraphia. The news wasn't easy to bear, but Ariana credits Barbara's guidance for dulling its blow. She placed Josh in a private school and enrolled him in after-school classes at Smarts 4 U. "Josh became a straight-A student," Ariana says with obvious pride.

When it came to pick a college, Barbara had a hand in that as well. She predicted that Josh would attend Berkeley, but that he would have to start school six months later owing to a shortage in student housing. Ariana hoped that she was right. At the time, Josh was adamant that he attend school in the east, far from California. For whatever reason, he eventually warmed up to going to Berkeley and, a short time later, it unfolded exactly as Barbara had said it would.

Josh graduated from Berkeley in 2002 in three years as opposed to the usual four. Josh plans to go to law school and has political aspirations. Lofty goals to be sure, but Ariana is convinced that had she ignored Barbara's advice and allowed the school to hold Josh back a year, he would have never excelled so far.

While Ariana and Josh credit Barbara for the way his life turned out, it wasn't always easy for Josh having a mother who was friends with a psychic. It's almost as if he's had two mothers with the added bonus of having one who knows everything that you're up to.

Ariana can recall an incident during Josh's first year at Berkeley with laughter and amusement. But, at the time, she was furious and panicked. While having lunch with Barbara one day, Barbara said, "We've got to talk about Josh. He's in some trouble and drugs are involved." Ariana immediately called Josh and a left a vaguely threatening message that must surely have struck fear into his heart. Ariana accused him of doing drugs but Josh was too out-of-sorts to argue and lamely mumbled that he was okay and that he didn't want to talk about it. That explanation wasn't good enough for Ariana. She and her husband drove up to Berkeley the next morning and as Barbara had seen, Josh had eaten five cookies laced with some sort of drug. He had spent the previous day curled up in his bed, hallucinating and vomiting.

Barbara continues to minister to Josh, though he may not always listen. Barbara believed that he would have been accepted into law school at Berkeley only if he had been willing to make some changes. Ariana charges that he didn't, and, as a result, is attending another school instead. A lesson was learned, however, and Josh is working hard with plans to transfer to Berkeley next year.

The Second Rung: The Husband
At her first reading, Ariana didn't want to know just about her son. She wanted to know if it was in her and her son's best interests to marry the older man in her life. Barbara had scribbled that this third marriage wouldn't be without its troubles, but that it would weather all problems and leave Ariana and her husband more in love with each other than ever. When Ariana saw how accurate Barbara had been regarding her son's learning disabilities, she began visiting Barbara more often, asking questions about her marriage, her husband and their future. The news was distressing, to say the least. The obstacles Barbara foresaw were daunting. She saw tragedy everywhere, especially when it came to her husband. He would fall gravely ill with prostate cancer in 1997. The illness would cripple the family financially but Ariana would make it all somehow work and they would get it all back. Her husband would lose his job in 2003, but he would find another and it was Barbara who would tell him how.

In 1996, Barbara told Ariana that her husband would develop prostate cancer and be unable to work. Ariana was devastated; she had everything that embodied the American Dream and was scared of losing it all. "I had the big house," she says, "the fancy cars. Barbara told me I would learn a serious life lesson." As overwhelming as the distressing news was, Ariana took comfort in the fact that Barbara said that they would be all right. She advised her husband that he should go see a doctor.

"My husband was always skeptical about Barbara," Ariana says. "He didn't share my beliefs and I learned from Barbara that what you said was sometimes not as important as what you didn't say." So Ariana didn't tell her husband that doctors would find that his cholesterol levels were off the wall, that his PSA levels were going to be stratospheric. Instead, he learned these on his own when he went to the doctor almost a year later. He learned that he had prostate cancer and his treatment schedule left him little time for work.

"Barbara predicted our financial troubles a year before they happened," Ariana recalls. "And she told me that when this time came, I would start selling things that I had collected to help us get by. She had no idea that I collected antique pottery and Barbie dolls." When the time came, Ariana did start an eBay business, selling the collectibles that decorated her home. She sold it all and lost almost everything. "It was a great life lesson, just like Barbara said it would be," Ariana says, looking back on those difficult times. "Everything just became…stuff. We lost a lot, but I realized…it didn't matter."

Her husband recovered and though the family had to move, they were able to afford a nice little townhouse in San Dimas. "In retrospect, you look back and you think,

'Wow. I wouldn't have made it without her.' Barbara guided us through it all—through his surgery and through his illness," says Ariana. She couldn't believe it all happened.

In early 2003, another of Barbara's predictions came to pass. At the time, Ariana's husband was working in San Diego during the week and returning to San Dimas on the weekends. When he returned home one day with a car laden with all his office possessions, Ariana wasn't surprised. Her newly laid-off husband was understandably troubled. "I'm 65, who's going to want to hire me?" he asked. With Barbara's words, Ariana reassured him that he would find something better.

A week later, Ariana's husband was offered a job that was pretty much perfect for him. When Ariana told Barbara the news, and she said, "This is the job for him. But it's going to be all about the resume. He's going to have to work on his resume." Barbara was exactly right. Three companies were involved in the hiring process, one of which felt that Ariana's husband would be a perfect fit for the position. There was a catch, however. To convince the other parties involved to hire him, the company felt that his resume needed some work. They had asked him to compress his 45 years of experience in the field into a manageable document. Ariana, who had come to see the accuracy of Barbara's predictions as a given, still found herself amazed at how closely events were hewing to Barbara's prediction.

A day later, Ariana's husband was procrastinating on the couch. Instead of working on his resume, he had settled down for an afternoon nap. The phone rang. Ariana answered and on the other end was Barbara, who simply commanded, "Tell your husband to get off the couch and go start writing that resume. He's wasting time." Ariana's husband sheepishly resumed his work. Everything was unfolding exactly as Barbara had said it would. "He was hired, he loves his job and most wonderful of all, he's living at home now," Ariana said excitedly.

Ariana still sighs when she thinks back on her marriages and is thankful for Barbara's insight. With two failed marriages by the time she was 28, Ariana had despaired of ever finding someone with whom to spend the rest of her life and she was happy that her third marriage was working well. Of course, not everything that Barbara told Ariana had a happy ending.

The Third Rung: Family

"I always had a feeling that I was going to end up alone," Ariana says softly, "but without Barbara to prepare me over the years for what was to come, I'm not sure I would have been able to remain sane. She knew that I would lose my family all within the same time frame and slowly helped me to cope with what was to come."

On Thanksgiving Day, 2002, Ariana had little to be thankful for. Her mother, after a brief bout with cancer, passed away. On March 2, 2002, her father followed. And, on Thanksgiving Day, 2003, her brother died. Her brother's death was especially hard to manage because she hadn't expected him to die so young, and at the time her husband was still battling his prostate cancer.

Barbara never explicitly told Ariana that her mother, father and brother would pass away. "I would have been devastated if she had," Ariana says. Instead, Barbara offered clues and directions, nudging Ariana towards the truth. A year before her mother's death, Ariana had made plans to visit Josh at Berkeley. She hadn't seen him for over six months and told Barbara how excited she was to take the trip. Barbara suggested that she change her itinerary and spend some quality time with her mother instead. At the time, Ariana wasn't terribly close with her mother and dismissed the advice. She could see her mother at the holidays, either Thanksgiving or Christmas, but Ariana never got the chance. Her mother passed away months later. With great regret, Ariana laments, "I should have listened. I was very aware then that I should have listened."

After her mother's death, Ariana forced herself to ask Barbara about her father. "Barbara," she asked, "my father is going to go right behind her, isn't he?" Barbara just nodded. A few months later, her father passed away. Though her brother's death was completely unexpected, Barbara had warned Ariana about her brother's gall bladder problems long before he died of a burst gall bladder.

With Barbara's guidance, Ariana was able to deal with many of life's major hurdles. She wonders what lies ahead for her for the next 10 years, and no doubt, Barbara already knows.

A Bright Light

Matthew was tired of life. Or so he thought. He woke up every day, stared morosely at his ceiling before rolling over and drifting off back to sleep. If he didn't sleep, then he just lay in bed, watching the television at the foot of his bed in a mindless daze. He flipped from one channel to the next. When he had run through all the channels, he just started all over again. If his housemates wanted him to go out, he begged off, saying something about having to study. But the truth was that Matthew had not gone to a class in months, so there was no studying to do.

His texts sat in a dusty heap on his desk among the debris of cigarette butts, empty liquor bottles and cellophane bags that once contained potato chips, peanuts or beef jerky. He didn't like going out anymore. For some reason, he was more than irritable these days and his sojourns to the bars usually ended with him storming off and locking himself in his room where he drank himself into a stupor. Everything seemed so utterly pointless to Matthew.

He felt alone and worthless. With a bottle of pills in hand and 13 ounces of vodka, he created a little cocktail for himself. The pills he crushed into a fine powder that didn't so much as dissolve but just floated in a dusty pale cloud in his glass. It tasted awful, but he continued to drink it. He thought about how his housemates wouldn't even notice his absence, how they would realize what had happened only when the smell of his decomposing corpse wafted out into the hallway. Then, maybe then, everyone would miss him and care about him. He drank it down and settled onto his bed to await death's arrival. When he woke up and found himself staring into a bright light, for a moment, he was convinced that he had arrived at the afterlife. And it was in that moment that Matthew suddenly regretted everything that he had done and wished he could change it all.

Hundreds of miles away from Matthew's apartment on Cottage Grove in Bloomington, Indiana, in the suburbs of St. Louis, Missouri, Matthew's parents were driving home from dinner. Their conversation over their meal of barbecued ribs had avoided the topic of their son, even though it had weighed so heavily on their minds. Both of them had noticed his drastic transformation.

Matthew had once been lighthearted and easygoing, but lately he was distracted, joyless and distant. They were worried about him and had even suggested that he start seeing a therapist. It was as if someone had replaced their son with someone else, but being hundreds of miles away, they had no idea how badly everything had regressed.

In the middle of the night, both of Matthew's parents woke with a start. They stared at each other in some surprise and both started talking about their unusual dream. In the confusion, neither one had really heard what the other was saying. They were just talking over each other before they realized that they had had the same dream. In the dream, both had seen Matthew curled up on the beige carpet of his bedroom. There was a disturbing stillness to his body; he looked wholly unnatural, like a slumbering statue. Both were certain that Matthew had done something drastic. The fact that they had both had the same dream only confirmed in their minds that their suspicions were correct.

They phoned Matthew immediately to make sure he was okay. It was a Friday night and they hoped that someone was home. There was no answer after the fifth ring, at which point the answering machine picked up with a recording of a far sunnier Matthew and his friends' comic message.

They hung up and dialed again. There was still no answer. Frantic, they didn't know what to do. They just kept dialing. Finally, after about 15 minutes of trying, Basil, one of his roommates, answered, and Matthew's parents were grateful that he was sober. He had just returned from the bars. Matthew's father pleaded with Basil to go check on his son. Basil, recognizing the gravity of the situation, did as he was told and with his cordless phone in tow, rumbled up the stairs to Matthew's room.

He pushed the door open and saw Matthew on the floor. The empty bottle of pills and vodka told Basil all he needed to know. Basil immediately called the paramedics and Matthew was whisked away to the Bloomington South Hospital. Matthew's parents huddled together and waited in agony for an update on his condition.

Matthew woke to a bright light. For a second, he wondered if he had entered heaven. He'd heard often about people seeing a bright light in near death experiences. Maybe this was the light they'd talked about. At that moment, Matthew felt the regret of a life unlived and realized that he still wanted the chance to live. He yearned for more life experiences. What a relief it was then when the bright light faded, and Matthew found himself staring into the eyes of a doctor.

As he was recovering his hospital bed, Matthew learned from Basil that his averted suicide had been nothing short of a miracle. Basil had only planned on stopping in the house just to change his beer-stained pants and then head back to the club. He doesn't know why he bothered to answer the phone, but he remembers a compulsion to do so. As for his parents' dreams, Matthew could only pause and wonder. It's a mystery he's chosen to leave unsolved. His parents accept it as a divine gift and another example of the Lord's mysterious ways.

Matthew, in the end, took his parents' advice. Though it pained him to do it, he entered counseling and through much introspection, support and guidance, he navigated through a very dark time in his life.

Psychic Doodling

Marty had always been a bit of a dreamer. Like most children, his mind drifted in classes. When teachers called on him, he stammered and muttered that he didn't know the answer. Shamefaced, he'd look down into his books and would often find there doodles that he'd sketched while gazing out the window. Doodling isn't uncommon; what was unusual about Marty's random drawings was that he was never completely aware of what he had been sketching. His own doodles were always a surprise to him, as if his pencil had been guiding his hand instead of the other way around. Even stranger, Marty had noticed that his drawings always seemed to have a habit of coming to life, as if they were visions of the future and not just random scratches on a page.

Usually, it would be something pretty mundane. For example, he would look down at his page after a couple of minutes of doodling and find that he'd drawn one of his friends getting kicked in the groin during a game of soccer. Inevitably, later, at lunch, his friend would get kicked in the groin. Or he might find that he'd drawn a picture of a friend kissing a girl he didn't recognize. And days later, when he saw his friend with a new girlfriend, she bore an uncanny resemblance to his sketch, Marty would have the strangest sense of déjà vu. He just thought that his drawing was just a case of spectacular coincidence. But one day changed it all, and Marty became convinced that no coincidence was at work.

He remembers that he was sitting in a math class about three years ago. Mr. Tompkins was lecturing in front of the class, as usual, in a nasal monotone about quadratic equations or something that might have sounded like that. The numbers on the board made no sense to Marty and for all he knew, he might as well have been looking at Sanskrit or Greek.

He let his mind wander, and as he did, so did his hand with pencil in tow. Marty scanned the room, from the clock above the board to his teacher's gnome-like face to the girl he had a crush on in the next row. When the girl caught his stare, Marty blushed bright red and quickly averted his gaze to his notebook. He gasped. His hand had doodled something completely unlike anything he'd ever drawn before. The image was horrifying.

It was a sketch of the very classroom he was sitting in, from Mr. Tompkins to the students sitting by the class-room door. The looks on their faces were ones of sheer terror. It was simple to see what had drawn their atten-tion. Half of the classroom was obliterated, obscured by lines of smoke and pillars of flame. Amid the fire was an automobile that apparently crashed through the school in a hail of brick and mortar and swallowed the lives of those in its path.

Marty just stared at the image. Something in his mind was telling him to do something, but what? He knew that urgency was critical, and he didn't have much time to act. And he had to resist his rational voice screaming, "Don't do anything, they'll think you're crazy!" Marty stood up and was about to begin yelling when he hit upon a better solution. He asked to go to the bathroom. The teacher nodded his assent and Marty left quickly. He ran down the hall and quickly pulled the fire alarm. Immediately, the halls filled with the cacophonous clanging of the alarm. He moved to the door and ran outside, praying that his classmates would soon follow. Pacing the front steps of the school, Marty wondered if he really was crazy. Of course, if he was wrong, no one would be the poorer for it. If he was right, then he didn't want to think about it. He breathed a sigh of relief when he saw the first students file out of the building. Marty was happy to see his classmates led by Mr. Tompkins.

Mr. Tompkins didn't look pleased. He barked at Marty to speak with him. Marty was only too happy to oblige. He looked over and grinned at his friends and was barely listening to Mr. Tompkins saying, "I presume that you didn't really have to go to the washroom?" Marty nodded absentmindedly. His attention was fixed on the road where an SUV was bearing down upon the school, swerving right and left with a high-pitched squeal. As the students of Marty's math class watched transfixed, the SUV jumped the curb that ran along the school's perimeter and barreled into the building with a huge, earth-shaking crash. Mr. Tompkins was dumbfounded. Silence fell upon the congregation. Marty was shocked that his drawing had indeed been a vision of the future. The SUV would have crashed right into him. Other students were shaking and whimpering at how closely they had been sitting to their deaths. The girl Marty had a crush on looked at him with a mixture of curiosity and awe, and he could only respond with a slight shrug.

In the aftermath of the bizarre accident, Marty learned that the driver of the SUV had had a massive heart attack while driving. He was already dead before his automobile smashed into the school. Though Marty would never receive official recognition for what he had done, it didn't matter. He may not have been able to save the driver, but he had saved many others, which was enough to give Marty satisfaction. He never really talked about his role in the incident, though the students of Mr. Tompkins' morning math class and Mr. Tompkins himself suspected, in some part of their minds, that they owed their lives to him. The class treated him with more respect after the accident. His crush was intrigued. She had seen the drawing on Marty's desk when he had left to go to the washroom, and Marty later confided in her about his premonition.

Marty still unconsciously draws images and objects. He does not to understand why he has this ability, preferring to just accept it as a fact of life. Lately, he hasn't been drawing anything that would prove terribly interesting to anyone outside of his circle of friends. For that, Marty is extremely grateful. And so is his new girlfriend, the girl from Mr. Tomkins' math class.

4

Danger!
Danger!

The Psychic Life

Ted doesn't sleep much because for him, sleep doesn't bring rest, but restlessness. To close his eyes is to invite the visions that have tortured him since he was a child. When he must sleep, when he's just too tired not to sleep, and he can't fight anymore, he reaches for the brandy. Maybe he'll drink one snifter, though on most nights, it's more likely to be three or four, followed by a prayer. "I pray," Ted says. "I pray that I may sleep in peace." He prays often, but most nights, his prayers will go unanswered. He will wake to a sunlit world that is harsh, glaring and drained of color, and his mind will be riddled with visions of the future that he must act on. "Sleep brings something that I will have to deal with," Ted says, "not because I have to, but because I am compelled to out of morality."

Ted can sense the future. He can sense death and tragedy. Some people may covet his abilities, but Ted sees them not as a gift, but as a curse. He struggles to make sense of his abilities. At 44, he doesn't remember exactly when it began, but it seems as if it has always been with him.

His earliest recollection was when he was four years old. He had spent an hour or so with his coloring books and became quickly bored with them. He looked around the room and saw before him a vast and pristine canvas of white living room walls. With crayons in hand, he eagerly began to draw. He didn't know he wasn't supposed to draw on the walls; he just wanted to keep coloring. His father had different ideas.

"My father was angry," Ted remembers. "As he walked up to me, he had a certain scent that frightened me." It was the first time that Ted realized that he had an acute sense of smell could detect mood, detect even the subtlest shift in temperament. "I learned early on," he says, "that certain emotions in people invoked certain odors. Fear and anger are very similar; they're both highly charged odors." Even individual people have their own scents "that separate them from each other." Ted can smell all that and more. He is a sommelier of emotion.

"My wife frequently gets upper respiratory infections," he says. "When she starts to come down with one, I can pick up the odor several days before it manifests itself. I can smell the infection." Ted can also smell death. Often, Ted has watched an ill friend speak hopefully about recovery and the future, only to sniff out the stench of death. All he can do to force a smile and nod. He knows it is wrong to rob someone of even the smallest hope. When Ted was five, his father died. For the young Ted, his father's death was sudden and unexpected. For Ted's mother, it had been inevitable.

A week before his death, Ted's father modeled for his wife his brand new Air Force uniform. She shuddered, wanting only "to scream at him to take it off." Two days before his death, Ted's mother was going to bed when she had a vision. As she stared at her husband's big toe protruding out from beneath the bed covers, she saw what she would later describe to Ted as a tag. She didn't understand its significance as a toe tag, but still knew that something dreadful was going to happen. The day he died, a rainy Saturday, Ted's mother had a dream. In her dream, the skies were raining blood. She woke up, and found herself in her husband's arms; she had been sleepwalking and he was just getting ready to go into the woods to chop some wood. She begged and pleaded with him not to go, but he shrugged her off. As she watched her husband walk out the door, Ted's mother knew it would be the last time she would see him alive.

Her husband didn't return. By evening, Ted's mother reluctantly telephoned the police and told them where they could find her husband's body. At the age of 47, Ted's father had died of a heart attack. He was buried in the brand new uniform that he'd shown off to his wife just a week before. Ted's mother was devastated. She had known he was going to die, but knew that there was nothing that she could have done to prevent it.

Ted missed his father terribly. He remembered how his father used to come home each night to read the newspaper, drink his coffee and smoke his cigarettes. He missed the aromatic scent of coffee and the sulfurous smell of the lit match and the woody odor of tobacco in the air. It was a routine that Ted associated with father. For half a year, Ted spent many nights crying in his bed, missing his father very much.

One night, Ted, inexplicably and suddenly, heard and smelled his father once again. He rushed from his bed and into the living room, but found no one there. It didn't matter though. Ted could sense his father's presence and he told his mother as much. She sensed it too. But his stay wasn't long.

Another evening, Ted was crying in his bed, wishing that his father could and would return. "Suddenly, I felt the mattress tip as though someone had sat down," Ted recalls. "I knew at that moment that he was with me. My sense of smell told me it was my father and I felt his love. I have never forgotten that night. It was the last time he came to me." Ted's father had come to say goodbye.

Ted never truly understood his mother's premonitions. A part of him was angry at her; after all, if his mother had been able to sense his father's death, then why hadn't she been able to do anything to prevent it? But Ted learned through a horrifying experience that it wasn't as simple as it seemed.

In the second grade, Ted had a friend named Edward. "We had always played together at recess," Ted remembers. "But on this particular day, something was different. When I saw Edward, I became very frightened. He came over to talk to me and I ran away from him. Something was very wrong with my friend. He looked strange. His head looked deformed. It was a Friday afternoon, and we usually walked home together, but as soon as the bell rang, I grabbed my coat and ran out of the building so I wouldn't have to look at him."

Ted spent the weekend trying to drive the image of his friend's grotesque head from his mind. But he couldn't. He was terrified. Deep down inside, he knew that something was wrong. The feeling sat in his stomach like a lump. On Monday morning, Ted went to class, fearing the worst.

"Our teacher announced that something very tragic had happened to one of us," he says. "Edward had been hit by a car and he had died. He died of head injuries on Saturday morning." In that moment, Ted understood. It was his (and his mother's) curse to see death's approach.

His mother told him that day when he came home from school, "Understand that most people do not know these things and that you must only communicate this with me and no one else. Because other people will not understand."

Compassion compels them to act and warn others of their impending doom. Sometimes, people will listen, and they can take some comfort in knowing that they have "saved someone from certain pain or death." But, then there are times when their warnings are dismissed with cynicism, and they must surely feel like Cassandra of Troy, the cursed prophetess, doomed to know the future but never to be believed.

When Ted was seven years old, his uncle and a friend came to take Ted fishing. Ted loved the smell of the lake, the sound of water lapping up against the sides of the boat and the peace of a leisure pursuit, but his mother refused to let him go. Ted and his uncle couldn't understand why and though they pressed his mother to explain herself, she refused. She just begged for his uncle not to go, but he was a stubborn sort, and he and his friend left anyway. "On the way to the lake, the car was hit by a logging truck," Ted recalls. "Although my uncle survived the encounter, his friend did not and was killed on impact. I would have been in the back seat. There was nothing left of the vehicle except the place under the dash on the passenger side where my uncle had wedged himself when he saw the truck coming." He should have heeded Ted's mother's warning.

"My mother can most often predict exactly what and when death will happen to someone," Ted says. "But I usually only know that something is very wrong." It's frustrating when Ted wakes with images in his mind that he does

Ted could smell a heavy scent of smoke in the air.

not fully understand. All he senses for certain is that "some type of terrible event will take place." It's like trying to put a puzzle together with only the faintest idea of what the picture is supposed to be.

During the night of September 10, 2001, Ted woke shouting from his bed. His nostrils were thick with the scent of smoke and his ears were filled with screams. He ran from the bedroom and grabbed a fire extinguisher. "All I could see was a wall of fire and people burning," he recalls. "The dream was so horrific and real. Later that morning, I realized its meaning." Like millions across the United States, Ted watched in horror as two planes slammed and exploded into the two towers of the World Trade Center in New York City. "I was afraid to go to sleep for nearly three nights after that," he says. "I was angry, too, because although 9/11 had been revealed to me, it was not specific enough for me to know what it meant." There are times, though, when Ted does see events unfold before his mind's eye and there are times, too, when he has been able to avert disaster.

Ted, like his father before him, served in the military. He speaks guardedly about his operations, as giving "unit names, dates and other information could seriously jeopardize their effectiveness in future operations as well as the security of military operations." Even without the fine details, though, Ted's story remains no less gripping or mystifying.

"At 0240, our team jumped into our zone," he remembers. "Our objective was reconnaissance. Our 12-man team was divided into three, four-man fire teams. We were armed with Soviet-made weapons so as not to be identified as

American soldiers if we were actually forced to engage. As I progressed, there was suddenly a familiar feeling of dread." Ted could sense that their mission had been compromised and that their presence had not gone unnoticed.

"My nose had picked up the scent of other soldiers on our trail and confirmed what I was sensing," Ted describes. "The enemy had our flank and was advancing rapidly." Ted quickly had his teammate radio their team leader, praying that he would listen to a man who was basing his opinion on nothing more than a smell and an intuition. He told his team leader that they had been spotted and that they not only needed to evacuate quickly, but that they also needed to use an alternate extraction point, because he "believed there was an ambush waiting for us." Ted's team leader listened and did as he had been advised. The team was evacuated without incident.

"Thank God he took my advice," Ted says. "We found out later that not only were we being hunted, but that one of our moles was actually a double agent and had tipped the enemy to our presence. They had been tracking our every movement. They had a company-sized unit waiting in place at our original extraction point." Ted's precognition and nose had saved his unit from disaster. There were questions, of course, about how Ted could have known what was waiting for them.

"When I was asked to explain my actions to command," he says, "I couldn't. All I thought to myself was 'Great. They're going to think I'm nuts.' But inexplicable as it was, the evidence was there and correct. And for some strange reason, I was now a sought-after member of any team. I got the job done sight unseen."

It's moments like these that Ted is grateful for his abilities. "This inner knowledge has guided me through life and it has saved me from things that could have taken me or those close to me," he says. "The reward is helping people go on because of the warning that they got from me." But still, there are the sleepless nights in which Ted sees only violence and destruction and feels a terrible burden that few can understand.

"I believe God gives us all something," Ted reflects. "But I am not sure that all of us are always ready for the things that are given. I hope one day I will fully grow to accept my destiny. Whatever it may be."

Party Premonition

Chelsea had long experienced premonitions and visions of the future. They usually dealt with minor things, but every now and then, she was presented with visions that had everything to do with life and death situations. The tragedy, as Chelsea sees it, is that she's often unable to act upon them. She would only see these events as they happened, not before.

One evening in the mid-1990s, Chelsea was home alone in her Los Angeles apartment. Her boyfriend Alex had decided to attend a house party with a friend and he'd asked Chelsea to come, but she had begged off. She knew no one there and she wasn't interested in spending her Saturday night with people in a keg line. Instead, she decided to relax with some music and read a book for the evening. She fell asleep with her cat in her lap.

Hours later, she woke up, still alone. Chelsea was disappointed that her boyfriend wasn't there. He said that he would come see her, but it was almost 3:00 AM. It wasn't uncommon for her boyfriend to abandon their plans, so Chelsea went to bed. She would simply call him later.

Chelsea woke an hour later with tears streaming down her cheeks. She wasn't aware that she had been screaming until she stopped. Chelsea was extremely disturbed by the nightmare that had roused her from sleep. She had seen flashing red and blue strobe lights from the ambulance and police cars. Her boyfriend had been shot and was being lifted into the ambulance. "It freaked me out," she recalls. "It was just so vivid." For the rest of the night,

Chelsea was on the phone, dialing and redialing her boyfriend's phone number leaving frantic messages. She never got an answer.

Chelsea sat down with a cup of coffee to wait for her boyfriend to return her phone call. The hours passed, and morning turned into noon and noon gave way to afternoon. Her phone rang twice; one caller had been her mother and the other had been a telemarketer. By late afternoon, Chelsea was very concerned and decided to call Alex's best friend Joe. She didn't know why she hadn't thought of it earlier, but she had been so intent on keeping her phone line free.

There was no answer at Joe's either. She called him repeatedly and finally got a hold of him. Breathlessly, she asked him what had happened the night before and whether Alex was all right. She described her dream and all that she had seen. Joe could barely utter a word. After a long pause, he told her there had been a shooting at the party last night. Everyone at the party had been detained by the police for hours, so in all the confusion and chaos, he and Alex were just released. Everything that Chelsea described had happened. The details that she had seen were eerily and uncannily accurate, except for one very important detail. Her boyfriend was fine, though he had been standing near the man who had been shot. Chelsea was relieved, but she still felt a chill. She'd never experienced anything like that before, and she was left wondering what the future might have in store for her.

Too Stubborn

Dave has always been eerily intuitive. Even from an early age, he can remember having vivid dreams that always had a peculiar way of coming true. As a child, he often saw figures that no one else could see. Dave still sees dead people. But as prescient as his dreams are, and as much as he's tried to prevent possible disasters and accidents, he still laments that people are just too stubborn to listen to his warnings.

His older brother Joe has always been reckless, impetuous and more than a little impulsive, whereas Dave, blessed with foresight and precognition, was naturally far more measured and practical—his parents were thoroughly relieved that at least one of their children used common sense and good judgment. Growing up, Dave had envied his older brother's carefree nature, so it was not surprising that many of Dave's earliest premonitions dealt with Joe. At the tender age of six, Dave warned his mother that Joe was up to no good in the basement and that she shouldn't have left him unattended with the iron. When she went downstairs, she smelled something burning and discovered that Joe had taken a hot iron to the carpet and scorched a hole into it.

Over time, Joe grew increasingly wary and tired of Dave's premonitions. He resented his little brother's meddling, and a rift grew between them. Often, he dismissed Dave's warnings and incurred a number of injuries, ranging from scraped knees to broken limbs, as a result. Sadly, Joe wishes now that he had listened to Dave's timely warnings.

Five years ago, Joe turned 16. It was a momentous day. He'd waited a long time to be 16 so that he could finally get a motorcycle licence. He had saved all the money he'd earned from years of allowances, mowing lawns, washing cars and pumping gas to buy a motorcycle. His parents insisted that Joe save his money, but if he was going to buy something, why not a nice safe little sedan? Joe wouldn't be deterred. He longed to feel the wind in his hair, to whip down the broad avenues and tree-lined boulevards of his hometown on a motorcycle.

Dave agreed with his parents. He knew it wasn't a good idea. One evening, he dreamed of his late grandmother, who had died when Dave was young. She came to him often in his sleep, usually to offer a warning. That night, once again, she appeared. She begged Dave to stop his brother from buying the motorcycle. "If not," she warned, "he's going to have a big accident in three months."

Dave, knowing that Joe would not listen, still pleaded with him not to buy the motorcycle. Predictably, Joe scoffed and laughed off Dave's warnings. "I'm learning from the best," he said. "I'm not going to be in any accident." Joe bought his motorcycle, with his parents' grudging approval. But there were conditions. He was not to ride at night and he was to learn how to control the motorcycle from a qualified instructor who met his parents' approval. He eagerly agreed to these concessions.

But, it wasn't long before he was paying only lip service to his parents' restrictions. Dave, for his part, tried his best to keep Joe off the road, but it was of no use. In no time at all, Joe was whipping around town on his motorcycle in rapture with the liberation that he felt at high speeds.

One month passed and then another passed, and it became clear to the few who knew Joe that he was a good rider, fundamentally sound and even talented. As the third month approached its conclusion, Dave hoped that maybe, this time, his grandmother had been wrong.

But one day, a phone call came when Dave and his parents were watching television. When Dave answered, one of Joe's friends described breathlessly that Joe had been in an accident and was in the hospital. Joe had lost control of his motorcycle and had been dragged several feet before coming to an abrupt stop by a fence. The good news was that his injuries weren't life-threatening. The bad news was that he had shattered his hip, and there was a possibility that he would never be able to walk again.

Dave remembers that Joe smiled weakly when he was finally lucid enough to see him. The jagged cuts and nicks were all over his face. Though in tremendous pain, Joe managed to utter, "I guess I should have listened to grandma." Dave didn't answer; instead, he just took Joe's hand and just held it.

Dave soon had another dream in which his grandmother appeared once again. She shook her head with tired resignation and said, "I guess he's learned his lesson now." Then she told Dave that he would need to help Joe stay strong and with time and a lot of patience and perseverance, Joe would walk again. Dave, who believed in the infallibility of his premonitions, did as he was instructed, even when it seemed as if the stress of Joe's rehabilitation would undo them both.

Their grandmother was right. Joe, with a lot of teeth-gnashing and cursing, did begin walking again. He still limps, a reminder, he says, to always listen to Dave and to be a little less stubborn. Dave laughs when he hears this, because it is so uncharacteristic of anything Joe would ever say.

Mother Knows Best

Joanne grew up watching the television comedy 'Father Knows Best,' but everyone in her family knows that it's not the father who knows best, it's the mother. Joanne's intuition has given her the eerie gift of foresight. Her family may not have initially believed in her ability, but it all changed a couple of years ago when they realized the full extent of her powers.

It was the end of summer and her daughter Gayle was due back at the University of Minnesota where she was finishing up her biochemistry degree with hopes of entering medical school. Gayle had wanted to fly back, but Joanne, feeling the desire to connect with her child, insisted that they drive from Chicago to Minneapolis. They would have over 400 miles of pavement on which to bond. Gayle wasn't exactly enthused about the whole trip, but at least she understood how important it was to her mother. She had spent the summer whiling away her days on Michigan Avenue and enjoying the sun in Grant Park with her friends. She had, admittedly, spent very little time with her family.

The drive itself was remarkably relaxed and blissful, devoid of the usual tension that both Joanne and Gayle experienced when traveling together. Joanne dropped her daughter off at her apartment building on Thornton Street and began the long drive back to Chicago. The sun was drawing near the horizon when Joanne drove away with one last wave.

Joanne returned to her home in Chicago's North Suburbs, greeted her husband quickly with a kiss before collapsing on the couch. She was relaxing with a glass of red wine when she sat up with a start. Something on her toe had caught her eye. It looked as if it had almost been severed. Blood seeped from a deep gash, almost obscuring what looked like a toe ring, and she swore she could see the white of bone. She gasped and reached for her foot, but when she touched it, she realized that her big toe was just fine. Frowning, she wiggled her toes, just to be sure. A toe ring? She didn't wear toe rings, but she knew her daughter did. Gayle had bought one only a few weeks ago. She knew instantly that something had happened to her daughter. Gayle was hurt somewhere in Minneapolis.

Joanne anxiously told her husband what she had seen, all of which he dismissed with a scoff and a puzzled stare. He told her not to worry, that she was just being paranoid and that Gayle was doing just fine. Joanne tried to accept her husband's pithy explanation for what she was feeling, but unfortunately, she found it impossible to concentrate on anything but her daughter. As the minutes ticked by, Joanne's anxiety only intensified. A voice in her head kept insisting that her daughter was hurt. To appease her, her husband called Gayle, but the phone just rang until the answering machine picked up. By now, Joanne was positive something had happened. Her husband remained calm; after all, school hadn't started yet and he was sure that Gayle was out with friends, catching up after a long four months apart.

Joanne sat by the phone, calling her daughter every 10 minutes, carefully punching the buttons and uttering a prayer as she did so. The phone still went unanswered. It was already late; it was 1:00 AM and Joanne was in a state of near panic. She had already made up her mind not to go to sleep until she heard Gayle wish her a good night. As she sat at the table, her head buried in her hands, the phone rang. She leapt to answer it and found herself speaking with a nurse from the Fairview-University Medical Center. The nurse explained that her daughter had had a little accident at a local bar. Gayle had cut her toe on some broken glass, but with a dose of antibiotics, she would be fine. Joanne breathed a sigh of relief and made a point to remind Gayle, again, about the perils of wearing sandals at bars.

Satisfied, Joanne thanked the nurse and went upstairs to wake her husband up. It had happened exactly as she had seen. Her husband, still heavy with sleep, was nevertheless amazed. He asked her how she could have known, but Joanne didn't know—it was just a feeling, a mother's peculiar intuition. No one in her family may be able to understand her abilities, but rest assured, her family no longer dismisses her warnings casually. Mother knows best, after all.

Father, Stay Home

Teddy's father had never liked the city much. It was why he was willing to commute to work and back, an hour or more each way, on a cramped and rattling bus from the bucolic, and though some might say dull, splendor of Katy, Texas to the cold, urban center of Houston. It was a long and arduous trip, but he did it every day, and sometimes reveled in the time he had to himself to read a book, listen to music or indulge in conversation with another passenger.

Teddy hated the suburban utopia to which his father had dragged their entire family. About five years ago, they lived in New Orleans, right in the city, where everything he wanted was never more than a few steps away. Here, in Katy, every house looked the same, as if Henry Ford had designed homes rather than his Model-T automobiles. The closest convenience store was at least a 30-minute walk away.

Ted longed to get on that bus with his father to go to Houston. Every morning, before he got dressed to go to high school, he watched his father with envy. *Someday*, he told himself, *I'll get on that bus and it'll be one way all the way*. Of course, after everything that happened in the summer of 2000, Teddy realized that he was no longer in a rush to get on that particular bus.

Everything changed for Teddy one week in July 2000. He was enjoying a nice, relaxing summer where he did nothing but wake up late, hang out with friends and go to bed long after the sun had set. But one Saturday afternoon, while playing basketball in the driveway behind his house with his little brother, he had a most peculiar vision. He remembers that he had the ball and jumped into the air for a shot when he saw something strange—scattered images flashed before his eyes like a fractured flip book. He'd seen a line of cars all jammed on a freeway. In the distance, he saw what appeared to be a huge accident. He thought he saw the flashing red lights of an ambulance and then the red and blue lights of police cruisers, but he couldn't be entirely sure. The next thing he knew, he'd missed his shot and the ball had landed in his neighbor's backyard.

For the rest of the day, Teddy was disturbed by the visions he had seen. The more he tried not to think about them, the more he did. Somehow, he felt it was a warning, but for whom and for what? The rapid-fire images left him with very little to go on.

The following day, he woke early, as the family always did on Sundays, to attend church and then go for lunch with the extended family. Teddy sat next to his father as he always did. It was an arrangement that had been worked out years ago so that his father could pinch Teddy whenever the boy's head started to droop.

Teddy listened to his minister preach about that week's topic and as usual, the dry delivery of the sermon made Teddy grow weary. In his dazed state, Teddy started seeing visions again, but this time, they were a little clearer. They still flashed before him in a rapid montage, but he could pick out the details. Faces were clearer—he saw women and men, bloodied and battered, struggling for life under the guidance of paramedics. Teddy realized one of the men was his father.

Teddy's visions of cars jammed on the freeway were too vivid to ignore.

It was all clear to him now. The accident involved the bus that his father rode every morning to work, and if his father got on that bus tomorrow morning, he would be in trouble. Teddy waited for more images, but a pinch from his father brought him out of his reverie.

For the next couple of hours following church, Teddy tried to speak with his father about his premonition, but he was far too busy speaking with relatives. Teddy didn't get his chance until late after they returned to their house in Katy. Teddy warned his father that he had a really bad feeling that his dad shouldn't go to work tomorrow. Teddy's father stared at him incredulously and told Teddy that he was being ridiculous. Teddy pleaded and pleaded, but his father didn't want to hear another word about it.

That night, Teddy set his alarm for 4:00 AM. He'd hit upon a plan to keep his father from getting on the bus. When his alarm rang, Teddy sneaked down to the front entrance and took his father's car keys. Without it, his father wouldn't be able to drive to the bus station today. Teddy happily crept back to his bedroom, leaving the door slightly ajar.

Later that morning, Teddy could hear his father shuffling around downstairs looking for the keys. He couldn't find them, and when he heard his dad grumble about having missed his bus, Teddy knew his mission was accomplished. His father woke Teddy's mother to drive him in her car for the next bus. Ted grinned and went back to sleep.

A few hours later, his mother woke Teddy. She was in a panic and told him that they had to rush to the hospital. She just received a phone call from the hospital saying that Teddy's father had been hurt in an accident on the freeway. He required multiple transfusions because of internal injuries, but he was going to be all right. Most of the passengers had severe injuries and there had been some deaths. "If only your father had found his keys," she said. Teddy stared, completely puzzled. Hadn't he averted disaster? He was stunned. After everything he had done, he realized that he hadn't prevented the accident from harming his father. He had seen the future, and there was nothing he could have done to change it!

Joyride

Carly never considered herself the sort of girl to shy away from anything. With three older brothers, she had always been a bit of a tomboy, preferring a good game of sandlot baseball to anything that the girls from her school were usually interested in. Her brothers had always challenged her with dare after dare and, eager to prove herself, she never backed down. She had an impetuous courage about her, and it was the sort of quality that endeared her to her friends. It was Carly who always came up with something wild to do on Friday nights, something beyond just renting movies and hanging out at the local mall. Carly was always about the good times, and under her direction, she and her friends made the streets of Cincinnati their own. Teachers sometimes called her a problem child, but that sort of criticism only boosted her standing in the eyes of her adoring peers. So naturally, it came as a bit of a surprise to her friends when they came to her one evening with an idea and Carly was the one who turned them down.

At the time, Carly was 15, with a bad reputation that had preceded her that year when she began high school. She did her best to live up to it. There were bush parties, flag pole stunts and a whole host of other things that she'd just rather not get into. It's a part of her that she's done her best to leave behind.

In early October, 2001, Carly was watching television when she heard a quiet knocking at the back door. She knew it was her friends because they had worked out a code long ago. Three of her friends were standing at the door with mischief in their eyes. One of them dangled a set of car keys in her hands before her. The girl had snuck out with her father's car. They spoke in hurried whispers, talking eagerly about driving down to the mall and cruising the parking lots. They were going to meet some older guys that they'd met that day in the cafeteria. It was definitely going to be a great time. Carly loved the idea. She told her friends to wait outside while she went to change.

As Carly was changing, her initial enthusiasm waned. Something inside of her was telling her that it wasn't a good idea—something terrible would happen if she went. She didn't hear a voice exactly. It was more like a mental push accompanied with a sense of dread. Shaking her head, Carly tried to dismiss it as paranoia, nothing more. Still, the sensation persisted and Carly found it impossible to exorcise, and then she saw the vision. In her mind's eye, she saw broken glass scattered across a road. She glimpsed at tangled seat belts, discharged air bags and her friends crying out for help. Such a thing had never happened to Carly before, and she knew then that she couldn't go.

Her friends were stunned. They goaded her, doing their best to persuade her to come. Was she scared of her parents? Or was she blowing them off because it hadn't been her idea? Carly just shook her head and told her friends not to go. "Something's going to happen to you," she said with such gravity that, for a second, it seemed as if they might actually listen. Carly's heart leapt, but for only a moment. Her friends looked at her, told her to suit herself and left.

Carly didn't sleep well that night. She just knew that something had happened to them. On Saturday morning,

Carly remembers being shaken from her sleep by her mother and father. Her friends' parents had just called, angrily demanding whether Carly had anything to do with what had happened. Her parents had to plead ignorance before they were told that the girls had indeed been involved in a car accident. They had managed to escape with just a few cuts, scrapes and a couple of broken arms, but the car was a complete write-off.

The news left Carly in a daze. She was so glad that her friends would be all right, but she wondered what had told her not to go and why hadn't she done more to stop her friends. She still has no answers. Instead, she's just accepted the event as something that just happened, for better or for worse. Her friends wished that they had listened to her and avoided the entire episode and its consequences—the injuries, the embarrassments and the guilt. Carly remains grateful for the vision. It is still a mystery to her, and in the aftermath, she found herself examining her life and her priorities. It led her to a long and sobering period of introspection from which she emerged wiser and certainly warier.

Baby Blues

It's never easy hearing that your unborn child may have developmental problems and severe disabilities. You only want the best for your offspring, and the very idea that they may, from the very start, be limited and subject to the prejudices and judgments of a largely ignorant society, can be daunting. Such was the scenario facing Anita when she was pregnant last year.

Anita was three months into her pregnancy when her doctor came to her with some grave news. He had looked over her family history and considering everything, had decided that Anita should undergo an amniocentesis. The procedure sounded simple enough. It didn't even require an overnight stay at the hospital or modifications to her diet. The doctor guaranteed that the pain would be minimal. Anita, as expected, asked the doctor why such a test would even need to be performed.

An amniocentesis, Anita learned, was performed to determine whether a fetus might have a chromosomal disorder, such as Down's Syndrome, spina bifida or anencephaly. Anita was more familiar with these terms, and the idea of an unhealthy child was completely frightening. Oh sure, she would love him as any other child she might have, but like any parent, she just wanted her child to be healthy. She agreed to the procedure. If it was bad news, she wanted the time to make the necessary preparations.

Like her doctor had promised, the procedure was simple. Indeed, it was the wait that would prove to be the more agonizing. Her mind had time to run rampant as it entertained all the worst and terrifying of scenarios. Her doctor told her that it would take at least 10 business days to get their results. Anita cast a glance at the calendar; she wouldn't hear anything for certain for at the very least two weeks. To Anita, it seemed as if it might as well be a life-time. It was a long time for her imagination to run amok.

Not a day went by where she didn't think about how her world would change if the results were positive for any genetic anomalies. She was all right during the days because she had things to occupy her time and mind. It was the nights, when she lay sleepless in her bed, that were the worst. With prayers running through her head, Anita was restless. Sleep usually did come, but only after three or four long hours of staring into the dark. A week of this torture passed and Anita just didn't know if she could handle waiting any longer. She was now becoming fearful of how her lack of sleep might affect her child. She didn't dare take any medication to help her sleep and nightcaps were out of the question.

But then, one evening, her salvation came. She had a dream in which she was giving birth to a son. The doctor delivered him, examined him and pronounced him healthy. Anita distinctly remembers being able to see her son's face and how calm she felt when she woke in the morning. She can't explain how or why, but she believed the dream was a premonition, a vision of the future and it told her that everything would be all right. It had given her an extraordinary sense of peace that she is almost at a loss to explain the sensation. Eeriest of all, Anita had pre-viously told her doctors that she did not want to know the sex of her child, but she was now positive that her baby would be a boy.

The next week passed and Anita spent it in relative peace and calm. Her insomnia passed and she slept, well, she slept like a baby. The tests were negative, as Anita had prayed for. Her baby was healthy. Half a year later, Anita gave birth and she recalls how strong the sense of déjà vu was when she did. It was as if she had experienced it all before, but it had happened in her dream. Her baby was a boy, as she had expected it to be. His face, his hands, his cry—they were all exactly as she had seen them months before. It was an experience, to be sure, that left Anita in awe of the unseen forces that she now believes directs human existence. "Never underestimate the power of a dream," Anita claims. "It can change your life."

A Skeptic No Longer

Fred had never been a psychic, nor did he ever want to go to one. It wasn't that he didn't believe in the phenomenon of ESP or telepathy or a sixth sense; it was just that he was positive that most of the self-purported psychics out there were frauds. And he wasn't going to give any of his hard-earned money to a fraud. So when the topic of psychics came up with his girlfriend one evening, she recommended that he go see hers because of how much the psychic had helped her and because the psychic offered a free first reading, but Fred was still skeptical and refused the offer. "I wasn't going to place my trust in just anyone," Fred says. "And my girlfriend, I always thought she was a little flaky. It's what I loved about her."

Though she pressed him to go, Fred remained steadfast. While he told her that he didn't want to get mixed up with such silliness, he never admitted the truth to her. He was scared. The idea that there actually might be someone out there who could gaze into his future and into his soul, exposing his deepest fears and secrets, terrified him. "I was blissfully ignorant," he says, with a laugh. "I just didn't want to know what she might see. It was as if knowing the future would take away all my hopes. I didn't want to know if I was going to fail at something or succeed at something. Uncertainty was kind of exciting."

But, in the end, his girlfriend's arguments won out. "It's free," she said. "You have nothing to lose, even if she's wrong. Which she won't be. And if she's right, you've everything to gain." He was finally cajoled into seeing the psychic.

He approached it with more than a degree of scepticism. All the talk his girlfriend had thrown at him about her career, love and family and how the psychic had spoken deeply and in great detail about it all without being told left him more than a little bored. It just wasn't that interesting to him. His girlfriend had told him to bring photos of the people he wanted to ask about, so he had, at the last minute, decided to bring one of his mother.

When he met the psychic, he was surprised. She looked and seemed so normal. There was no crystal ball, nor were there tarot cards. There were no muttered incantations or spells. She spoke plainly, uttering nothing about auras and chakras. And he had to admit that she was pretty detailed in everything she said. He allowed grudgingly that maybe she was the real thing.

When he showed her the photograph of his mother, she gasped slightly, as if she didn't like what she saw. "Is she ill?" the psychic asked. Fred smiled. He had her. At last, she erred. His mother wasn't ill. She had had a physical the year before and the doctors had pronounced that she was in good health. The psychic shook her head and insisted that Fred take her to a specialist. "She's ill," the psychic continued. "She's got problems with her uterus. She will need to see someone soon, and she will need a hysterectomy." It sounded serious. Fred paled a little, but still he had just seen her and she was fine. He recovered his composure and told the psychic that she had to be wrong. The psychic did not say anything further. She just smiled and let Fred go on his way.

His girlfriend took the news quite seriously, insisting that he should do as the psychic recommended. "She's fine," Fred insisted, irritably. Hadn't he done enough to humor both the psychic and the girlfriend? He couldn't believe that his girlfriend was taking the psychic seriously.

A week later, he went to visit his mother. He greeted her and despite his doubts, he found himself looking her over, searching for any indication that she might be sick. His mother noticed that there was something different about his mood and asked him what it was that was bothering him.

He laughed and proceeded awkwardly to tell her about his visit with the psychic and what she had told him. When he was finished, his mother appeared stunned. Fred rolled his eyes. *What was it with women and psychics*, he thought to himself. But it was Fred's turn to be stunned.

His mother went on to tell Fred how she had had an appointment with her doctor. She had been experiencing some unusual symptoms lately and wanted to make sure that she was all right. Her test results would be ready in the following week.

A week later, Fred found himself anxiously waiting for his mother's call, to hear what the doctors had to say. It was already 3:00 PM and he should have heard from her. He paced the floor rapidly, frustrated that he had allowed this psychic to get to him so easily. The phone rang and he answered it breathlessly. It was his mother.

As the psychic had said, she would need a hysterectomy. Doctors had found cancerous tumors in her uterus, and a full hysterectomy was needed to remove them. Fred felt as if he had been struck with a baseball bat. His stomach twisted, his legs grew shaky, his heart pounded. Would his mother die? He'd known many people who had lost their lives to it, and he wasn't ready to lose his mother to it, too.

His mother seemed in good spirits. "The doctors caught it early enough, they think," she said brightly. "I'll be fine. I'll only be in the hospital for a couple of days and then I'll be home. Apparently, it's a pretty simple procedure and I shouldn't worry." Fred wasn't mollified, and ironically, he returned to the psychic for more information. "Yeah, my girlfriend loved that I asked to see the psychic again," Fred says. "I'm just grateful that she never actually said, 'I told you so.'"

At his second meeting, Fred just wanted to know if his mother would be all right. He breathed a huge sigh of relief when the psychic nodded that she would be. Fred wasn't fully convinced that the psychic was 100 percent accurate, but at the very least, her words gave him some sense of peace and calm.

It was a sunny day when Fred's mother went into the hospital to have her operation. Fred was with her, having taken the day off from his job. He remembers pacing anxiously in the hospital waiting room, trying to convince himself that the sterile scent that surrounded him wasn't the scent of death. He did his best to ignore everyone around him—patients who were connected to oxygen tanks with tubes protruding from their noses and their bodies frail and gaunt beneath the pastel greens of their gowns—and instead, he focused again and again upon what the psychic had told him. It became his mantra for the duration of his mother's operation and her recovery.

In the end, Fred needn't have worried. The psychic was right, and after a couple of weeks of bed rest, Fred's mother was finally up and about once again. She suffered no ill effects from her operation. As for Fred and his scepticism regarding psychics, it has been exorcised. He speaks to his psychic regularly and for a time, he was consulting her on every little detail about his life. Recently, he asked her whether his girlfriend would accept his marriage proposal. The psychic laughed, smiled and said plainly, "You don't need a psychic to answer that." Fred and his kooky girlfriend are engaged. His mother fully plans on attending their wedding next year. The psychic said as much.

One Shirt, Two Shirt, Blue Shirt

Martha was always a cautious mother. When her son, Adrian, was just a baby, he suffered inexplicable seizures for which the doctor could offer no diagnosis. When Adrian was two, the seizures inexplicably stopped. Martha never stopped worrying, however, always wondering when the next one might come and always dreading that when it did, it would take her son's life. Those precarious early years instilled in Martha a need to protect her son in everything that he did. She became overbearing and cautious.

As a result, her son led a sheltered existence, unable to participate in any of the activities that his friends took part in regularly. When he was younger, Adrian didn't seem to mind. He read voraciously, often wrote stories and printed his own newspaper. When he wanted to play a sport, his mother enroled him in tennis because she believed it was a sport in which injuries were uncommon. As Adrian grew older, he became unwilling to accept his mother's precautions.

He railed against her rules and regulations, and when he broke them, arguments and shouting matches ensued. Adrian longed for a chance, for once, to do all the things that his friends were able to do—to play soccer, football and hockey. What did he do? He just sat in classrooms or his bedroom, and it had become all so horribly mundane. His mother refused to sign permission slips allowing him to play on any sports teams, refused to buy any equipment for said sports and when Adrian appealed to his father, all it took was one quick stern glance from Martha to silence him. She thwarted him at every opportunity and finally, Adrian gave up asking her.

Adrian's friends loved mountain biking. Living in Washington, Adrian found that routes were plenty and varied. Adrian knew that his mother would detest the idea of his cycling on river valley paths, but found a way around her wishes. When he bought his bike, he told his mother that he just wanted to exercise. He would stay only on well-lit streets, always wear a helmet and promised to never ever take it off the road. Martha was just grateful that he'd finally given up on the idea of football and hockey. In her mind, biking was a safe activity. The roads of their suburban neighborhood were broad and traffic was never heavy. She insisted that he buy a bell, but Adrian put his foot down when she suggested that he also buy a flag.

For months, Adrian rode his bike in and around the paths of his neighborhood, developing an intense love for the sport and demonstrating an innate talent for it. He began to tackle increasingly complicated routes and was grateful that the scrapes and bruises could be easily hidden beneath long sleeve t-shirts and trousers. His mother never suspected a thing. But if it hadn't been for his mother's timely intervention one late summer day in 2003, Adrian might never have lived to tell his tale.

Adrian graduated from high school in spring of 2003 and was spending his last summer eagerly preparing to attend the University of Missouri at Columbia. He was going to study journalism, and though he knew that his mother fostered his love of both communication and the written word, he never would have admitted that much to her. When he wasn't working at the community paper, Adrian was off on his bicycle, navigating with the greatest of ease paths that had once seemed so daunting. Martha remained blissfully ignorant.

But one evening, Martha had a frightening dream. She saw an accident in which a car hit two people on bikes. From her vantage point, Martha couldn't identify who had been hit. All she could say with any certainty was that the individuals, both bearing a resemblance to her son, were wearing blue t-shirts. The dream played again and again in her mind until she finally woke. It had felt unbelievably real and for a second when she woke, she was convinced that it had all happened. Only when she reminded herself that it had been a dream was she able to relax. Well, for at least awhile.

The following afternoon, Adrian had plans to get together with his friends to do some biking. Adrian greeted them at the door and then ran upstairs to his bedroom to change his clothes. He threw on a ratty pair of shorts and pulled a t-shirt over his chest. Satisfied, Adrian bounded back down the stairs where he found, to his dismay, that his mother was having a conversation with them.

He didn't mind his mother talking with his friends, exactly. It was just that she could be so bizarre, often jumping without reason from one topic to another. And, there was the fear that one of his friends might very well slip and let her know where they planned to go that afternoon. Martha was startled when she saw him. Adrian stood before her, glaring slightly at his mother, in a blue t-shirt. She commanded Adrian to change his shirt and

That afternoon, Adrian just wanted to go biking without his mother's knowledge.

insisted that he couldn't leave the house unless he put on something else. Adrian, puzzled, did as he was told. If he were to protest, he might very well lose the entire day. He bounded back down the steps, clad now in a green t-shirt with the logo of some obscure local underground band. Martha smiled and looked over his friends. With an almost inaudible sigh, she was happy to notice that none of Adrian's friends were wearing blue. She said her good-byes, told the boys to be careful and then watched as they sped away on their bikes.

The afternoon passed without incident and as the day wore on, the temperature continued to rise. One of

Adrian's friends was wearing a jacket and probably would have taken it off earlier if only his friends hadn't goaded him about it. They'd said that he would be too hot but he wasn't going to give them the satisfaction of knowing that they were right. It was petty, he had to admit, but now, he was sweltering with his clothes clinging to his body, so he relented. He removed the jacket, revealing a sweat-stained blue t-shirt underneath.

Their ride was at an end and they were riding back to their homes when a girl approached and stopped Adrian. His friends continued along their way. Adrian recognized the girl from his school, but until now, had never had a conversation with her. He returned her smile with an awkward look to which she said, "Hey, where'd you get that t-shirt? I've been looking for one just like that for ages." Adrian spoke to her for just a few minutes and continued on his way. He pedaled quickly to catch up with the others but didn't have to go far.

Just around a corner, he saw his friend in the blue t-shirt lying on the road. His bicycle was more than a little mangled. His friend lay in a crumpled heap while the others hovered around him. He had been hit by a car backing out of a driveway. The car had rolled over his bicycle, but luckily, his friend managed to move clear from its path. The driver was aghast.

Adrian's friend suffered a broken ankle, but other than that, escaped from the accident relatively unscathed. The driver, in the end, bought the boy a new bicycle, and though some people may have pressed for a lawsuit, his friend chose forgiveness instead.

Adrian's mother was stunned. She knew then that her vision had indeed come true and that she had protected her son from harm. If only she had told them all about what she had seen, then perhaps his friend would be fine. When she asked Adrian if his friend had been wearing blue, Adrian thought it a very strange question to ask, at least until she explained why. When she did, he suddenly remembered that he too had been wearing a blue t-shirt and how he had changed t-shirts. He recalled how that girl had stopped him to compliment him on his new t-shirt and how this delay more than likely saved him from harm. Adrian never thought it would have been possible, but for once, he was grateful for his mother's zeal for excessive caution.

5
Farewell To Thee

A Mother's Farewell

Sunny had never met her father. He'd packed his bags and split for Montana even before Sunny was even born, leaving Sunny's pregnant mother alone with her parents in San Diego. They weren't thrilled, but they didn't mind too much having Sunny's mother with them. Sunny's father was an abuser who would hit her mother when arguments got out of hand. The two had just never got along. So, for the first 14 years of her life, Sunny never knew her father. He was just someone her grandparents and mother seldom talked about. Still, even knowing what she knew, Sunny couldn't help but wonder who and what her father was. It was only natural. All her friends had mothers and grandparents, but they also had fathers. Where was hers? For the most part, she loved her life in San Diego. She had doting grandparents and a devoted mother. And then, in 1981, when Sunny was 14, she took a trip that would change her life forever.

"I will never forget the feeling I experienced on the night of June 25, 1981. I had left San Diego by plane to go to Montana to meet my father and his family for the first time," Sunny recalls. Her mother had urged Sunny to take the trip, even if she did worry that Sunny might never want to come back. That night, in her father's basement, Sunny tried to sleep. It had been a busy day. She had just met her father along with her stepmother and three new half-siblings, two young sisters and a young brother. And while her father had been gentler and kinder than she had expected, her stepmother could have stepped right out of

Cinderella. She was particularly unkind and cruel, insisting that she wanted Sunny to have nothing to do with "her and her family." It wasn't exactly the warm reception Sunny'd hoped for.

Still, there was something else that disturbed Sunny. Something deep in her mind nagged at her, though she didn't know exactly what it could be. She hadn't slept for long when she was startled by something in the room.

"I was awaken by the distinct feeling that someone was standing at the foot of my bed, staring at me," Sunny says. "I thought it was one of my siblings, checking out their big sister. I sat up and asked, 'Who's there?'" She kept her tone friendly but received no response. In the darkness, she couldn't see anything at the foot of her bed, so she turned on a light. There was no one there, but the feeling proved too strong to ignore. Sunny searched the basement, expecting to find a half-sister or half-brother giggling in the shadows. She even peered beneath her bed, but found nothing under there but dust bunnies that scurried away from her. Puzzled, Sunny simply shook her head, turned out the light and went back to bed. As she drifted back into sleep, Sunny felt someone sit down on the side of her bed. She could almost feel the person, pressing against her. Slowly, she opened her eyes and saw nothing. It was the strangest thing. The feeling was so strong and pressing that Sunny turned on the light again only to find herself alone.

"I wasn't scared," she recalls, but she was certain that something had happened.

In August, Sunny returned to San Diego. It was only after she had returned to her grandparents' house that she

Memories of her mother continue to remind Sunny of her inherent abilities.

understood the truth behind what had happened that first restless night in Montana.

With tearful eyes and voices choked with grief, Sunny's grandparents told her that her mother had passed away. She had died the very night that Sunny had left. Though heartbroken, Sunny felt an odd sense of peace because she knew that a part of her had known that her mother had died. The late-night visitor she'd received in her bedroom in Montana was her mother, who had come to bid a last farewell to her daughter.

Her grandparents had delayed passing the news to Sunny because they didn't want her father gaining custody of her. "I wasn't upset that they waited so long to tell me," Sunny says. "Grandmother always did the right thing." They needn't have worried. When told of the death, Sunny's father originally accused Sunny of being a liar and only backed off when he was sent a copy of the death certificate. "Even then," Sunny says, "he didn't attempt to gain custody. His wife had convinced him that I was bad."

Sunny and her father, estranged for so many years, finally began speaking again in 1999. They had run into one another at a conference in Dallas, Texas, and though he didn't recognize her, Sunny had still said hello. In the intervening years, Sunny was surprised to see how closely her life mirrored her father's. "We both graduated from college with identical degrees for elementary school teaching," she says, "and we both ditched the idea and ended up in the exact same business of advertising specialties. The convention in Dallas was also a trade show... turns out I was his main vendor, and he was one of my company's best distributors. We're almost identical in nature. In my mind, the nature versus nurture controversy has been settled." Yet, she still wonders if a psychic connection with her father exists, as it did with her mother so many years ago.

A Death Foretold

When Todd was a young boy, he lived next door to Mr. and Mrs. Christie. He first met Mr. Christie when he was five, and Mr. Christie, though only in his late 50s, seemed ancient. Mr. Christie had been raking leaves in his front yard, smoking a pipe. He introduced himself as Mr. Christie, at which point Todd was convinced that he was living next door to the famous Mr. Christie, the one who made "good cookies." He was wrong, of course. It was his wife, Mrs. Christie, who made the good cookies.

Todd spent many an afternoon at the Christies, and they were glad to have him. They had no children of their own and probably thought of themselves as his second parents. After all, the Christies were close with Todd's parents, having met them on the day that they had first moved into the house next door. When Todd was six, they moved away. His mother and father felt that their small house wouldn't be large enough for the brood that they planned to have.

Though they didn't move far away, it was far enough that Todd rarely saw the Christies. His parents had dinner with them often, but Todd only saw them on odd weekends and holidays. Mrs. Christie always brought over some cookies on their visits. In time, Todd saw less and less of the couple. If he did see them, it was for only a few seconds before he was out the door, rushing off to meet his friends. Still, Todd remembered them fondly and always made a point of asking his mother and father how they were doing.

After graduating from college, Todd left his home-town, returning only at Christmas and Thanksgiving.

Sometimes, he would see the Christies, but they were getting older and increasingly fearful of driving, so they preferred to spend their days at home on their sun-drenched patio after a long day of gardening.

When Todd was in his early 30s, he returned home for Thanksgiving. Feeling nostalgic and eager to show his fiancée where he had grown up, Todd and his parents went for a drive around their old neighborhood. It was amazing how much the street had changed, but it was still comfortingly familiar. Their old house was still there, though its stucco façade had been replaced with vinyl siding. Todd smiled when he saw how large the maple tree that he tried to uproot as a child had now grown. He once towered over its branches, but now, the tree soared high above the house.

As their car went past the Christies' home, Todd remarked on how sad it was that Mr. Christie had passed away. His mother and father looked at him with surprise; as far as they knew, he was still alive and well. They had even called ahead, to see if they would be free, but as luck would have it, the older couple were out of town visiting friends. Todd shook his head, a little confused, until he remembered that Mr. Christie had only died in a dream that he had had the night before. He had seen Mr. Christie, much greyer now, but still vigorous and hardy, walking towards their old yard in a dark, three-piece suit. Todd was standing in the yard, watching. Mr. Christie saw him, smiled and then waved, not as a greeting, but as a farewell, before disappearing. His parents told him that he must have confused his dream with reality. The explanation was logical enough. Still, he remained convinced that his dream meant something more. If Mr. Christie wasn't dead, then he probably didn't have much time left to him.

The following day, Todd and his family learned exactly how prescient his dream had been. Mrs. Christie telephoned and broke the news that her husband had indeed passed away, just the day before. His funeral was to be held in a couple of days, so Todd extended his stay.

At the funeral, a viewing of the body was held. Todd's fiancée chose not to go in with him. While she waited outside, Todd and his family walked in, heads bowed and hearts heavy. When Todd peered into the casket, he gasped. His mother, noticing his reaction, asked if he was all right. He nodded quickly before turning to his parents and whispering, "It's the same suit. It's the same suit that I saw him wearing in my dream. I don't believe it." Todd took one last, lingering look at Mr. Christie. He was clearly shaken by what he had seen. His dream hadn't just been a dream; it had been a premonition. Todd had foreseen Mr. Christie's death.

Though the premonition left Todd with questions about the possibilities of a psychical world, it also gave him peace. In his dream, Todd remembered most vividly how at ease and serene Mr. Christie had been. Todd had seen a man ready for death, a man who had lived long and done all that he had wanted, without any regrets. When Todd spoke with Mrs. Christie at the wake, he mentioned the dream and what he thought it meant. Mrs. Christie, smiling as tears ran down her cheeks, nodded with comprehension. It turned out that she too had seen her husband in a dream and was very pleased that he had gone to see Todd as well. It was Todd, in the end, whom Mr. Christie had always thought of as the closest thing he would ever have to a son.

A Grandfather Says Goodbye

Bob and Jeanie Harris, like all couples, will always remember their wedding day. They will always remember the toasts, the presents and the vows. To be sure, everyone had a wonderful time. Guests made full use of the open bar, the food was excellent and everyone present agreed that Jeanie and Bob made a beautiful couple. But for Bob and Jeanie, they'll also remember the day because it was the last time they would ever see Jeanie's father alive—and because he told them so.

"My father was a healthy man and still relatively young," Jeanie recalls. "So when he came to me at the end of the night and said, 'Goodbye, Jeanie. I hope I get to meet my grandson,' I laughed and stared at him." She thought her father was being ridiculous and told him so. After all, she was already pregnant, and his grandson was due in just a few weeks. He smiled and looked at Jeanie with clear blue eyes that were rimmed with tears. A chill passed through Jeanie's body. "My father wasn't what you would call an emotional man," she says. "It was the only time I'd ever seen him cry."

Her father continued to speak, and told her a story about something that had happened just a few nights before. He had been asleep in bed when he suddenly woke up. Lying there in the darkness, he felt there was someone else on the bed. He could feel its weight, and though he immediately thought that there was an intruder in his home. His initial fear was quickly replaced with a sense of peace. In the feeble light of his table lamp, Jeanie's father saw, sitting on his bed, the apparitions of his late wife and brother. They looked at him, spoke gently and said, as they receded into the darkness of the night, "You'll be with us soon." The story finished, he turned to his daughter and pulled her head close. He whispered into her ear, "I know I'm dying."

Jeanie was incredulous. Her father had always been the most reasonable and practical of men, always dismissing accounts of the paranormal as ridiculous flights of fancies related by bored housewives and stoned teenagers. "I suppose that's why the story left such an impression," Bob says. "The very fact that he believed it…if anyone else had told him the exact same story, he would have just dismissed it."

Bob and Jeanie asked their father to stay with them in Atlanta. After all, they were moving into a newly built home shortly after the wedding and there was more than enough space to accommodate him. But he refused. He didn't want to be a burden and only wanted to return to his house in Tallahassee, where he and his wife had spent more than 30 years together. "He told me that if he was going to die," Jeanie says, her voice breaking slightly, "he wanted to die at home. There was nothing else we could do."

Jeanie wanted desperately to visit her father, but doctors advised against her traveling so close to her due date. And she needed her rest. The couple had many sleepless nights. "Our telephone was always ringing at two in the morning," Bob says. "And the strangest thing was that the voice mail wasn't picking up. It just kept ringing and ringing until we answered it, and then all we heard was a dial tone. There was never anyone on the other end." They called the phone company to see if there was anything wrong with their line and their voice mail, but the technicians told them repeatedly that there wasn't. The mysterious calls continued unabated.

Their son was born a month later, on September 13, 2001, a few weeks premature. Jeanie and Bob had hoped to travel to Florida soon after, to introduce their son to his grandfather, but it was impossible. He was simply too young, too small and too fragile for travel. In fact, they were only able to bring their child home a month after he had been born.

"That first night," Bob says, "that's when it all happened." Bob and Jeanie were ecstatic to finally have their son home. His bedroom, which they had painted blue and filled with all sorts of toys and mobiles, had sat empty for too long. With their son nestled snugly into his crib, the room now felt alive, full of warmth and love, as it should be. Exhausted, Bob and Jeanie crawled into their bed and drifted blissfully off to sleep.

A few hours later, they woke up when their dog started barking at something in the baby's room. "We couldn't see anything," Jeanie says, "but the dog was growling and baring his teeth, and usually he only does that when the mailman or strangers come to the house." Their son woke and began screaming, terrified, no doubt, by the large creature barking just feet away from his crib. The din was only amplified when the phone began ringing. Bob and Jeanie looked at one another and then at the clock they'd hung in their son's bedroom. It was 2:00 AM.

"I was so confused," Jeanie recalls. "The dog barking, my baby crying… it didn't even register in my mind that my husband was actually speaking on the phone." She turned to her husband, who was speaking in hushed tones. He nodded every now and then, but with each passing moment, his posture seemed to sag more and more. He hung up the phone and sadly turned to his wife. The dog had stopped barking.

Jeanie knew from the look in her husband's eyes that the news couldn't be good. And deep within, she knew what had happened. The question lay flat and thick upon her tongue and she didn't want to ask it, as if her silence might turn back the hands of time and postpone the inevitable.

"It was my sister," Jeanie says. "She was calling to say that our father had died just a few hours ago from a sudden heart attack." She remembered everything her father had said at her wedding and then remembered his wish. He had said, "I hope I get to meet my grandson." Everything suddenly became clear. The barking dog, the mysterious phone calls that came at 2:00 AM—Bob and Jeanie were convinced that they were connected to Jeanie's father.

"We sincerely believe," Bob says, "that her father came to us that night to see his grandson. We believe and know that he got his wish and that he died happily." After that night, the phone calls stopped and though Jeanie lost her father, she feels that he is somehow always with her, that he continues to watch over her and that even death can't dull the power of his love for Jeanie and his new grandson.

Dance of the Fireflies

Philip will never look at fireflies the same way again. They are now symbols of an untimely death—of loss, misery and sadness. When he sees fireflies glowing and shimmering like some earth-bound constellation of stars over a darkened field, he's flooded with memories of his brother.

Three years ago, when Philip's brother was alive, Philip woke up one evening in his Ann Arbour apartment with a terrible feeling. It set his heart racing. It sent a shiver through his body and his breaths became short and ragged. Panic coursed through his body in waves and Philip sat up in a cold sweat. He'll never forget the feeling. It was as if needles were racing through his veins. As he sat there, trying to regain his breath, Philip knew that someone close to him was going to die.

He splashed cool water on his face and went out onto his balcony for a breath of fresh air. As he stood there, wrapped tightly in his bathrobe, Philip saw hundreds of fireflies swarming above the ground. It was a constellation of twinkling lights like Philip had never seen before. The swarming fireflies emitted a soothing glow that bathed their surroundings in a pale neon light. Philip watched in awe, nearly forgetting what had sent him out onto the balcony in the first place. The feeling of dread returned for an encore, only this time, it was stronger and far more intense. The fireflies' glow became frightening to Philip, so he retreated into his bedroom and tried to fall back asleep.

Over the next couple of days, sleep proved elusive. Every night, he would wake with the weird sensation that

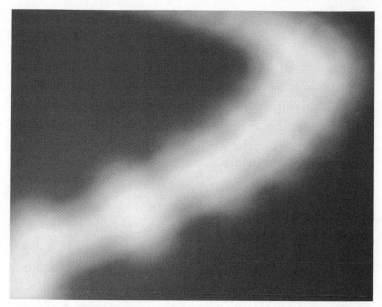

Philip was overcome by the wondrous glow of the fireflies.

someone close to him was going to die. And every night, he would pad out onto his balcony and see the fireflies. He saw them in his dreams, on his way to work, on his way home from work and any time he went out for a walk. He'd seen them before, but never with such frequency. It was as if they were trying to send him a message.

A week later, Philip received a call on his cell phone from his father. His father's voice sounded hoarse, so Philip knew that he had been crying, and he sensed that he had terrible news. Philip's brother, Curtis, who was living in Grand Rapids, Michigan, had passed away. He had died of a massive heart attack and his body had been found by his 10-year-old daughter, Elise. The news was devastating because Philip and Curtis had been extraordinarily close.

He realized that his premonition was correct; death had indeed been stalking someone close to him. Philip stood at the window of his apartment and looked out onto the grounds. Oddly enough, Philip noticed the fireflies were there again, shimmering and sparkling, in full force.

The funeral was held days later. With a heavy heart, Philip drove to Grand Rapids and tearfully embraced his mom and dad. He took his niece, Elise, in his arms and looked into her tear-stained eyes that resembled so closely her father's. He lamented that Curtis would never meet her first love, would never see her graduate from school and would never walk her down the aisle on her wedding day.

The wake was held at Philip's parents' spacious house. The rooms were full of guests dressed in shades of black. Conversations were punctuated with laughter and fond memories of his brother. It all became just too much for Philip to bear, and he escaped onto the back veranda. It was cool there, and the night was dark with a cloudless sky above. He gazed up at the stars, wondering if his brother could see him. He was distracted again by a swarm of fireflies, but this time, their light was enveloping a small figure. Amid the fireflies was Elise, who was trying to catch them with her small hands. She looked so serene in her playfulness. The lights fascinated her, and Philip watched her with a mixture of relief and sadness. Her smile, more radiant now than the luminous tails of the fireflies, comforted him.

Philip now understood that the fireflies were sending him messages. The fireflies, with their eerie and mysterious yellow-green glow, were not only the harbingers of his brother's death. They also reminded him that Elise was the beacon of hope for the future.

Mother, Mother

Lynn will always remember the day her mother began her steady march towards death. It happened on a September afternoon five years ago. It was the day that Lynn first heard the voice. It was only the beginning of a series of unexplained events that would culminate in her mother's final words. These words were whispered to Lynn, not in the hospital room where her mother lay in a coma, but in Lynn's own bedroom as she slept.

The day had begun like any other. Lynn's mother had gotten up early, padded out of her bedroom in her slippers and bathrobe and made breakfast for Lynn's two young sons. Lynn woke up to the smell and sound of sizzling bacon and made her way to the kitchen where she asked if her mother would be willing to watch her children for the day. Her mother agreed because she loved watching the two boys. They made her feel young, she said.

Lynn planned on spending the day with her sister-in-law, Bonnie. They were going to go furniture shopping for the new house that Bonnie had just moved into, have some lunch and then watch a movie. Lynn was relieved to have a chance to spend some quality time with an adult and talk about something other than whatever fad it was that her children were interested in talking about. She said goodbye to her mother and her children and then went on her way.

Lynn and Bonnie spent the day as planned and returned to her sister-in-law's for coffee before catching a matinee. As Bonnie wondered what film they should see (either *Shakespeare In Love* or *Saving Private Ryan*), Lynn suddenly felt a compulsion to go home. It was as if an inner voice inside her head was telling her to go. Lynn shook her head, ignoring the voice and told her sister-in-law to choose the movie. Still, the voice persisted only with greater urgency.

The voice was insisting that Lynn go home immediately. A sense of dread was beginning to creep into her consciousness—something terrible had happened at home and she needed to go. She left her coffee unfinished and stood up quickly to pick her coat up from a chair and her keys from the table. Her sister-in-law stared at Lynn, puzzled. "The movie isn't starting for another couple of hours," she said. "What was the rush all about?"

Lynn apologized, wishing she could offer Bonnie a better and more rational explanation but it was beyond her. Lynn left and raced back to her house as quickly as the speed limit would allow. She returned, ran through the garage and into the house. Her sons were standing at the door confused and scared. "Grandma fell," they said. Lynn brushed past her children and into the kitchen. Sprawled out on the tiled floor in her bathrobe was Lynn's mother. Lynn shook her, but she was just lying there still and lifeless with her eyes closed.

Lynn called the paramedics, hoping that her mother would regain consciousness soon. The paramedics arrived and sped her to the hospital. An anxious Lynn bundled her two sons into her car and followed behind the ambulance.

As she waited in the waiting room, doctors examined Lynn's mother. The news was far from good. Her mother had suffered a massive stroke. She had slipped into a coma and doctors were unsure if she would ever regain consciousness. Lynn remembers the hospital waiting room swirling around her and the floor buckling beneath her as she listened. Her mother was dying and she might never even get a chance to say goodbye. When she entered her mother's room, she could hear the slow, wheezing rasp of the ventilator that was breathing for her mother. Lynn watched her mother for a moment before sitting down in a chair next to the bed and taking her mother's hand. She started talking anxiously to her aloud about everything— her children, the room, the television and the doctors. Lynn sat with her mother until the end of visiting hours.

Though her mother never responded, Lynn firmly believes that she heard every word that Lynn said. For the next week, Lynn made a daily pilgrimage to the hospital. For as long as she could, she sat next to her mother and said all the things that she wanted to say to her mother. Mostly, she told her how grateful she had been to have a mother like her and how much she loved her. Lynn's mother continued to lie in the hospital bed motionless. Her body seemed to be evaporating, growing frailer and smaller as the days passed, as if her life were slowly seeping from her.

Two weeks after her mother's stroke, Lynn was asleep in her bedroom and dreaming. In her dream, her mother appeared before her in a form that Lynn could scarcely remember. Her mother was svelte and thin, looking very much like the mother who had raised Lynn during her earliest years. Lynn was walking towards her mother in her dream, and she knew that her mother would be leaving soon. Her mother reassured Lynn that she was happy and that she had lived her life long enough. She said goodbye and then disappeared.

Lynn woke up abruptly and looked at the clock—the bright red digital numbers flashed 9:00 AM even though it was not yet dawn. Puzzled, she went to sleep again until the phone rang later that morning. It was the hospital calling to inform Lynn that her mother had passed away at 9:00 AM. Lynn felt not regret, but peace. The dream had given her solace. Her mother had come to say goodbye, and Lynn knew, beyond a doubt, that her mother was content and in a far better place.

The Hitchhiker in the Road

The night was dark and the road was long. Liza was feeling drowsy and had already caught herself nodding off a few times when her car rattled its way over the rumble strips along the Ohio highway. On some level, she knew that she should just pull over and take a nap, but she told herself that she would be home soon enough. She rolled down her window, hoping the briskness of the night air would help her shake off the overwhelming fatigue. She put in a CD, a loud rock album with screeching vocals and guitars, and turned up the volume to the point where the bass rumbled in her speakers. She felt confident now that she could stay awake for the rest of her journey.

It had already been a long day. She had woken up early in the morning, much earlier than she was used to, and made the long drive from her home in Columbus, Ohio to Indianapolis, Indiana. Almost everyone from her mother's side of the family was there, having come from all across the country to visit her sick aunt who was trying to recover from a lengthy illness. She had been ill now for months, and though no one said it, it was clear to everyone that she didn't have long to live. It was the reason why Liza had decided to drive the three hours to Indianapolis. She knew that it might be the last time she would see her aunt alive.

The day had gone well. The family had met at her aunt's nursing home where a small reunion was being held in the basement cafeteria. Her aunt was in a wheelchair, no longer strong enough to walk with her cane. She was frail and small, much more so than Liza could recall. Her cheeks were sunken and her skin looked like aged parchment. She was quiet for most of the time, nodding at faces that she recognized, frowning with frustration at the ones she didn't. Liza said hello but she was shocked to see that her aunt didn't even recognize her. They had always been close and Liza had often been told that she was her aunt's favorite niece. Instead, she just muttered and asked who the pretty girl in front of her was. When she was told, her aunt just frowned and shook her head. A short time later, she insisted that she be taken back to her room. She was tired and wanted to sleep. Everyone bid their clumsy farewells and she was wheeled back the way she had come. Liza waved goodbye, but wondered if her aunt even noticed before the doors closed with a decisive thud.

The rest of her family stayed on in the cafeteria, making polite yet forced and meaningless conversation that made Liza uneasy. These people may have been her family by blood, but they seemed to be strangers now. She wanted to flee as soon as her aunt had, but she felt obliged to stay. Finally, after a few more hours of awkwardness, Liza felt comfortable enough to tell everyone that she was leaving. Some people suggested that she should at least stay for some dessert, and even invited her to stay in their hotel rooms. Liza insisted that she had to get back to work early the next day.

Now, as she drove east towards Columbus in her somnambulist state, a part of her wished that she had stayed. Even with the chilly night air and the blaring music that threatened to deafen her, she could feel her eyelids drooping. From behind her half-opened eyes, she saw a figure dart right into the path of her car. Liza shrieked and slammed on her brakes. Her tires squealed in protest. She cursed and honked her horn. Standing there in the spotlight of her headlights was a woman. She looked old and frail and even from the car, Liza noticed that she bore an uncanny resemblance to her aunt. But it couldn't be her. Her aunt was all the way back in Indianapolis, tucked in her bed in the nursing home.

Liza got out of the car and approached the figure slowly. The closer she got, the more the woman looked like her aunt. The woman could have been her aunt's twin. "Are you all right? Would you like a ride?" Liza asked. The woman didn't answer. Instead, she just stood there, with her eyes closed. Liza asked her questions again, but again, the woman stayed silent. "I'm going to get help," Liza said, turning back to her car to get her cell phone.

"No," the woman said. "Wait. I just want to say one thing." The woman had opened her eyes, but there was nothing behind her eyelids save for two dark and empty sockets. Liza very nearly jumped out of her skin. "Goodbye," the woman said. Liza was horrified and sprinted back to her car. She grabbed her cell phone, but when she turned back, Liza saw nobody standing there. The woman was gone.

Liza drove away, wondering whether everything that she had seen had just been a bizarre dream. Had she, in her exhausted state, imagined it all? She had looked around for the woman. After all, the woman was old and frail and couldn't have gone far. But Liza found nothing to suggest that the encounter had ever happened. All that she was left with was a deep confusion and sense of overwhelming dread.

She returned to her condo in Columbus exhausted, wanting nothing more than to take a warm shower and go to sleep. Wearily, she entered her home and sighed loudly when she noticed the blinking light on her answering machine. It was flashing repeatedly with new messages. It had to be her family—only they would refuse to ever call her on the cell phone. Her mother and father left messages for her to call them as soon as possible.

It wasn't unusual, of course. Liza's parents always worried about her driving late at night and probably just wanted to be sure that she had gotten home all right. The hour was late, but Liza dutifully called her parents. They told her that her aunt had passed away during the evening and wondered if she would return to Indianapolis in a couple of days for the funeral. The news wasn't a surprise to anyone. Her aunt had lingered on for far longer than anyone had thought possible. For Liza, the news left her wondering if her strange encounter on the highway had greater metaphysical significance. She would have told her parents about it, but they were practical, reasonable folk who would have scoffed at her story. Even she was growing more and more convinced that she must have imagined it all.

A couple of days later, Liza drove back to Indianapolis. She thought about what had happened as she drove past the stretch of road where the encounter had taken place. In the light of day, she could see the skid marks her tires had left. They gave Liza a chill.

At the funeral, she saw many of the same faces from the nursing home. Even more family had flown out now, and Liza saw cousins and relatives that she no longer recognized. She was grateful for her parents' company as they made the rounds. They knew everyone, recalling names and occupations with ease. When the service began, Liza noticed that her aunt's casket was closed. She asked her mother why.

"It's because of your aunt," her mother whispered. "She donated her corneas and, well, she has no eyes. Everyone thought that this would be best." Stunned, Liza asked her mother to repeat herself. "She donated her corneas, dear," her mother whispered. "They took out her eyes."

Liza sat in silence. The old woman hadn't been just a figment of her imagination. She knew then that the old woman had to have been her aunt, appearing one last time to say "goodbye" to Liza. Later, Lisa learnt that her aunt had died some time around 1:00 AM. Liza couldn't be certain, but she was pretty sure that she had seen the woman at about the same time.

Liza misses her aunt still, but remains grateful that she came to say goodbye. She remembered the love and closeness that they had once shared together. It was a small comfort, but Liza tells herself that her aunt is no longer in pain and that she must be in a better place. Liza swears that there are times when she can feel her aunt watching her from above. She never did tell anyone about the encounter, not even her parents. She wants to keep that memory for herself.

Signs

When his son Josh died, Tony was devastated. Yet, at the same time, he was far from surprised. In the days leading up to Josh's sudden and inexplicable death, Josh acted as if he knew the end was near. Tony remembers thinking the behavior was just a little odd. It frightened him, but he just assumed that it was all just a phase, or maybe it was some kind of strange new fad among the kids. He didn't know and just hoped that it would pass in time. It didn't, however. Josh passed away from a seizure on October 27, 1995.

It was early morning and, as usual, Tony had gone to wake up his son, who was notorious for waking up late and arriving at school even later. He found Josh on the floor, dressed in his green hospital scrubs and red Indiana t-shirt, and though it was a little curious, he didn't think anything at all was amiss. He called out to him and shook his shoulders, but Josh didn't respond. His body remained limp. Tony called Josh's name again, but there was still no response. Panicked, Tony ran out into the hallway to call 911.

The paramedics arrived quickly and they did their best to revive Josh at the home. Their efforts were futile. The paramedics rushed Josh away into the ambulance and Tony and his wife followed in their car. After an hour of wild oscillations between hope and despair, Josh's parents learned that their son had passed away.

The funeral arrangements were simple to make. Josh had made it clear what sort of funeral he would like. He had told his father what sort of casket he would like, what music he wanted to play and who he wanted to speak. It seemed most bizarre to carry out a funeral planned requested by his son, but Tony made sure all Josh's requests were met.

Weeks after the funeral, Tony finally allowed himself to enter his son's room. He looked with pain at the spot on the carpeted floor where he had found Josh. It was the last time he had seen his son alive. He opened drawers, rifling absentmindedly through papers and books. In the dresser, beneath neatly folded clothes, Tony found a box. Within the box, he found a tattered leather-bound journal. He recognized that the journal had been his gift to Josh just a few years before. Tony had always assumed that Josh had thrown it away or given it to someone else, but his son had actually made use of it.

Feeling guilty but wanting desperately to breathe life into his memories, Tony began to read Josh's observations—his own exhortations to resist the downward pull of negative self-esteem, his crushes, his friends, his hopes and dreams. Tony realized, gratefully, that he knew, at least to some extent, variations of these stories. Sure, he didn't know all the details, but the heart and soul of the accounts were the same. He had had a better relationship with his son than he thought.

But as Tony continued to read, he noticed that Josh wrote less and less about his life and more and more about his death. It was in these entries that Tony glimpsed a side of his son that he had never known about. His son wrote about dark dreams and terrible visions that plagued him both day and night. They had begun a month before his death and it was clear from the journal entries that his son was terrified. It would explain the sudden shift in his mood and temperament.

His first dream had come at night and had disturbed Josh enough for him to wake up and write about it. The entry was dated September 27, 1995, and had been written at 3:00 AM. In it, Josh asked one question over and over, his handwriting growing more frenzied each time he wrote it. "What does this all mean?" he wrote. Josh went on to describe the dream in great detail.

Josh had seen everything unfold before him as if he were just a floating spectator. He was hovering above his bedroom and below was his body curled up in a little heap at the foot of his bed. Below him, his bedroom door opened and Tony entered. Josh had written that his father had rushed over and gently shook him. Josh didn't respond. His head just lolled on the floor, and Tony grew more agitated. As Josh watched, his father placed a finger on his wrist, checking for a pulse. There was obviously one because Tony looked up to the heavens with gratitude and then he ran from the bedroom.

Josh's mind had captured every detail. He noticed that he had been wearing his usual pajamas, hospital scrubs and a red Indiana t-shirt. His radio was tuned to the local Top 40 station and its assortment of loud and obnoxious DJs. Judging from the amount of sunlight in the room, Josh had guessed that it was early in the morning. He'd waken, bathed in sweat, just after he watched his father leave the room.

The next entry, from the following night, described how Josh had tried to forget the dream but had failed. It had occupied his every thought, and he was growing more panicked by the day. He wrote about how he wished he could tell someone who could understand. Unfortunately,

Josh planned all the details of his funeral well in advance.

he couldn't think of anyone who would fit the bill. Tony grimaced. Josh was right; Tony was one those people who wouldn't have understood. He had always dismissed the existence of ghosts, wraiths, goblins and anything that could be deemed paranormal or supernatural. Tony shook his head and continued to read.

As the days progressed, Josh's entries became more desperate. He was having the dream regularly, except now he got to see his father return to the room. Paramedics inevitably followed, at which point he watched himself being whisked away from his room. The dream always stopped there and Josh wondered what would follow. Sometimes, he was optimistic, but he was becoming progressively pessimistic. He had written again and again, "I think I'm going to die."

In the last few entries, Tony noticed Josh's growing obsession with the numbers 10 and 27. Josh had written how he was seeing those numbers all the time; he would look at the clock in class, and it would read 10:27. He would be waiting to catch a bus and he would see the 10 and the 27 pass in quick succession. When he was in his room, listening to music and reading, if he glanced at his clock, he always seemed to do so at 10:27. He didn't know what the numbers meant, but Josh was convinced that they meant something. Tony sighed. He had the benefit of hindsight and knew exactly what those numbers meant. His son had died in the 10th month on the 27th day. Tony tried to grasp the implications. His son knew that he was going to die, even down to the day.

The final entry, dated October 26, was long and rambling. It seemed that Josh had written through the night, in an attempt to transcribe all his ideals and beliefs. He was, in essence, preserving his spirit and soul with the written word.

When Tony finished reading his son's journal, he understood why his son had outlined his funeral plans. Tony often wonders whether something could have been done if he had known of his son's death in advance. Maybe doctors could have discovered the defect that had claimed Josh's life. Tony doesn't know what would have happened and tried not to torture himself about it. Josh's journal now occupies a special place on Tony's bedside table. Its pages, he admits, are stained with tears.

The End